THE BOB HOPE FILMS

THE
BOB HOPE
FILMS

by James L. Neibaur

McFarland & Company, Inc., Publishers
Jefferson, North Carolina, and London

ALSO BY JAMES L. NEIBAUR
AND FROM MCFARLAND

*The RKO Features: A Complete Filmography of the Feature Films
Released or Produced by RKO Radio Pictures,
1929–1960* (1994; paperback 2004)

Tough Guy: The American Movie Macho (1989)

Movie Comedians: The Complete Guide (1986)

BY JAMES L. NEIBAUR AND TED OKUDA
AND FROM MCFARLAND

*The Jerry Lewis Films: An Analytical Filmography
of the Innovative Comic* (1995)

Frontispiece: Bob Hope.

LIBRARY OF CONGRESS CATALOGUING-IN-PUBLICATION DATA

Neibaur, James L., 1958–
    The Bob Hope films / by James L. Neibaur.
        p.   cm.
    Includes bibliographical references and index.

    ISBN 0-7864-1050-7 (softcover : 50# alkaline paper) ∞

    1. Hope, Bob, 1903–[2003].   I. Title.
PN2287.H63N45   2005
791.4302'8'092 — dc22   2004026710

British Library cataloguing data are available

Cover photograph: Bob Hope in *The Big Broadcast*, 1938

Manufactured in the United States of America

McFarland & Company, Inc., Publishers
    Box 611, Jefferson, North Carolina 28640
    www.mcfarlandpub.com

For Mom,
who said she always liked
Bob Hope

Acknowledgments

The author wishes to thank Ted Okuda, Gary Schneeberger, Jerry Mathers, Phyllis Diller, Jerry Lewis, the late Buster Crabbe, Dick Cavett, Woody Allen, Brent Walker, and the people at Bob Hope Enterprises for their help.

Contents

Introduction

Bob Hope started out in show business while still in his twenties, remained active past the age of ninety, and lived to celebrate his hundredth birthday. His longevity is remarkable, especially when one considers that his career spanned vaudeville, radio, motion pictures, and television. He excelled in each.

While there are transcripts of his radio shows and existing clips from his television work, these are more likely archived in museums and other cultural centers. Few are readily available. It is unlikely that these would be representative of Hope's career.

His films, however, are genuine testaments to his timeless comedy. His smart quips, fast pace, and breezy manner were perfect ingredients for the sort of comedy that was popular during the war and in the immediate post-war years. The Bob Hope films from 1942 to 1952 are uniformly among the best comedy features of their time.

As a 1950s cinematic style developed, Hope's successes on screen became more sporadic. By the 1960s, his films often appeared woefully out of touch.

Contemporary critics have occasionally complained that his best films, including *Road to Morocco*, *My Favorite Brunette*, *The Princess and the Pirate*, and *The Paleface*, often relied too heavily on topical humor that does not always withstand the test of time. Hope kidding about his radio sponsor being Pepsodent may have been amusing when he was heard over the airwaves in households across America each week, but many of today's critics argue that these dated lines hamper the effect of the films.

Perhaps.

It can also be considered that many entertainments of the past are, in and of themselves, cultural artifacts. The topical references contained therein are part of the cultural experience of understanding, even celebrating, past achievements.

None of the Bob Hope films are classic comedies in the same sense as the groundbreaking achievements of Charlie Chaplin or Buster Keaton. Hope was not a filmmaker. He was, instead, an eminently likable and talented comedian whose film appearances offer the sort of light escapist fare that equaled tremendous box office success during wartime and its immediate aftermath, when war-weary Americans needed the sort of breezy comedy Hope offered.

In this film-by-film account of Hope's movie career, there isn't anything of substance to discuss about the camera, direction, or mise-en-scène. There is, however, a great deal to say about what was genuinely funny and what remains every bit as delightful many decades later.

Hope's film career can be categorized fairly easily. Not counting the handful of two-reelers he made during the early 1930s, his feature film career starts, appropriately, with The Beginning (1938 to 1940). It was during this period that Hope established himself on screen. He started out as just another brash, amusing comic presence in a handful of entertaining B pictures. His radio success prompted his studio, Paramount, to try him in an A picture, *The Cat and the Canary* (1939), which Hope always recalled as pivotal in taking him from the lower to the upper level of double bills.

The second period is the Starring Years (1941 to 1952) when he was a bonafide box office star, resting comfortably among the top ten draws among American movie stars. It was during this period that Hope appeared in his best films. Nearly every movie he made during this section of his career not only was a box office smash but has withstood the test of time exceptionally well.

Then came the Uneven Years (1953 to 1960), when Hope made some good comedies (*Off Limits, Casanova's Big Night, Alias Jesse James*), some successful experiments with more serious roles (*The Seven Little Foys, Beau James, The Facts of Life*), and some unfortunate misfires (*Here Come the Girls, The Iron Petticoat, Paris Holiday*).

During the period we can label The Final Years (1961–1972), Hope made his weakest films, including *Critic's Choice, Call Me Bwana, The Private Navy of Sergeant O'Farrell*, and his last, *Cancel My Reservation*. Attempts to address the generation gap in *I'll Take Sweden* and *How to Commit Marriage* presented Hope, and his writers, as woefully out of touch. Adult romantic farce (*Boy, Did I Get a Wrong Number!*) and family fare (*8 on the Lam*) were mildly amusing, but only in comparison to the doldrums of the other movies Hope was appearing in at this time.

It isn't difficult to understand why Hope's success in movies did not last. This is to say his critical success, as even his weaker films of the 1960s managed to turn a healthy profit. As Hope got older, he had difficulty finding an image that was as amusing as his cowardly, phony-bravado, girl-chasing wiseacre from the 1940s and early 1950s. Presenting himself as a staid conservative family man beset by generation gap troubles merely helped relegate him to Hollywood's old guard. Forced sitcom-level comedy hardly seemed relevant during the era that gave us such innovative films as *Bonnie and Clyde*, *The Graduate*, and *Midnight Cowboy*.

Too many baby boomers, coming of age during Hope's least interesting cinematic output, recall only his weak efforts and his pro–Vietnam hawkishness during a very sensitive time in our recent history. (It is an amusing irony that the even more notoriously right wing W. C. Fields was embraced by boomers for his iconoclasm during the late 1960s.) However, now, in retrospect, it should be rather easy to celebrate Hope's wisecracking, fast-paced, delightful films during his best period.

By the time Hope reached his one hundredth birthday, many top stars acknowledged how much his easy manner influenced their own styles. Woody Allen has long made it a point to praise Hope's comic method as a strong influence on his own. An Allen film like *Love and Death* owes a great deal to Hope films like *Monsieur Beaucaire* and *Casanova's Big Night*. Allen himself has admitted that his fondness for the murder-mystery comedies, such as *My Favorite Brunette* and *The Great Lover*, helped to inspire his own film *Manhattan Murder Mystery*.

Actors and comedians like Kelsey Grammer, Conan O'Brien, Jay Leno, Dick Cavett, and Drew Carey have all admitted to using elements of Bob Hope's masterful delivery and sense of timing to enhance their own work.

Bob Hope's films capture his classic comic style on many levels. While some of his later films appear dated and tiresome, most of his work remains exciting and relevant.

This book will look at the Bob Hope films, but not with the same sort of analytical approach one would offer the work of Ingmar Bergman or Federico Fellini. The Hope movies do not have deep subtexts or clever cinematic innovations, but the best Bob Hope films are clever, uplifting entertainment packages that not only inspire carefree laughter decades after their initial release but offer us some solid examples of what made the American home front smile during the second world war and helped heal us during its aftermath.

It is unfortunate that so much of cinematic study relies heavily on film's artistry and therefore overlooks some of the real talent that put out pure entertainment product.

Perhaps the height of this unpretentious style occurred during the 1940s and early 1950s during which Hope was doing his best work. Abbott and Costello, Red Skelton, the Three Stooges and Danny Kaye were also active in films and offering some of their most timeless efforts. None of these comedians appeared in movies that can be embraced as great cinema. All of them, however, offered comedy that has lasted far longer than so many of the era's pretentious epics.

From the films of Bob Hope, we can see all of the basic elements that make a good comedian — his timing, delivery, style, and commitment to the material. When all these elements gel, the results are quite wonderful.

The Early Career
of Bob Hope

Leslie Townes Hope was born in England on May 29, 1903. As a child, Hope was fascinated by comedians in silent movies, particularly Charlie Chaplin.

Chaplin was, at this time, the biggest star in the world and the first really enormous star that the fledgling film industry had known. His films remain staples of cinema's development, and his contribution places him as perhaps the single most important figure in the history of motion pictures.

Chaplin's popularity was so tremendous that movie marquees would simply advertise "He's here!" Audiences would flock to the theater in droves and pay full admission price to see a twenty minute comedy run endlessly.

Hope's connection to Chaplin was instrumental in his showbiz career. It is frequently noted that his first professional gig was a Chaplin look-alike contest he won as a child.

Another of the more amusing tales about Hope's youth was that he worked as a boxer, Packy East, prior to entering vaudeville.

Upon embarking on a show business career, Hope tried his hand at doing a dance act that was augmented by smart quips.

One of Hope's first big breaks came in the touring company of "Hurley's Jolly Follies of 1925." This show was produced by Fred Hurley. Hope and his partner, Lloyd "Lefty" Durbin, had performed in a review featuring Roscoe Arbuckle and it is he who introduced them to Hurley.

Arbuckle who, as the beloved Fatty, had delighted audiences in silent pictures only five years before, was amused by the young two-act and decided to give them a leg up. Arbuckle had been one of silent cinema's finest comedians and would likely have emerged to deserve an honored place alongside the likes of Chaplin, Buster Keaton, and Harold Lloyd had a 1921 scandal not ruined his career. On the boards, his name still meant something. His

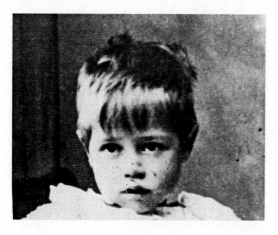

Hope was born in England but came to America as a child.

connection was so beneficial that Hope remained grateful and would acknowledge Arbuckle decades later.

The Jolly Follies played smaller towns for about a year, and the experience was invaluable for Leslie Hope. Hurley followed that show with "Hurley's Smiling Eyes," but while touring in production, Durbin collapsed on stage. The cause turned out to be tuberculosis. Lefty died in a Cleveland hospital soon after.

Hurley then hired dancer George Byrne to replace Durbin. Hope and Byrne became fast friends and worked very well together.

Hope and Byrne played in various vaudeville and review shows throughout the 1920s, essentially maintaining a dance act but with very little comedy. They opened in a Broadway show, "Sidewalks of New York," in the fall of 1927, but their contribution was minimal and they were soon released.

While appearing in a small-time vaudeville show, Hope was asked a favor by the theater's manager. Once he and Byrne finished their dance act, would Hope come back out and announce the show that was to appear the following week? Hope agreed.

Once he and Byrne finished and left the stage, Hope strolled back out and addressed the audience. "Ladies and gentlemen," he said, "next week there is going to be a *good* show here!" It got a laugh, so Hope made a few good-natured jokes about the act that was to perform there the following week. The laughs continued and the manager noticed. Throughout the engagement, Hope would make the announcements once he and Byrne had finished and would keep adding jokes. It got to the point where he was doing four or five minutes of closing material.

Hope realized he could succeed on his own as a master of ceremonies, but he was apprehensive about breaking up the act with Byrne. He recalled how Byrne stepped in and saved his career when Lefty Durbin died and how the two of them enjoyed a special rapport on stage and off. Byrne, however, realized Hope was too good for a two-act and gallantly stepped aside. Byrne eventually opened a dancing school. He and Hope remained friends until Byrne's death.

As the 1920s became the 1930s, Hope's vaudeville career maintained a steady level of success. As an emcee he was funny, charming, and likable. Soon he was in demand and appearing at top vaudeville spots such as the Palace. By this time, Leslie Hope was being billed as Bob Hope. There is no solid explanation for the name change. Hope has stated over the years that he felt the first name Bob simply sounded friendlier and more accessible.

In 1933 Hope was hired to play the role of Huckleberry Haines in the Broadway musical "Roberta" which became a big hit. When the show ended, he returned to vaudeville as one of its highest paid performers.

Hope's success during this period offered him some minor opportunities in movies.

Even though Hope's very inauspicious film debut was in a handful of weak short subjects and his initial feature films ranged from guest shots to larger roles in smaller movies, his tenacity and appeal soon allowed him to emerge as a top motion picture star.

The short films seem terribly unfunny today and are interesting only because they represent the early work of so important a comedian as Bob Hope. Even in these unremarkable efforts, however, there is a clear sense of style that is impossible to ignore. Even period critics noticed that Bob Hope wasn't merely another snappy smart aleck. He had a personality that audiences realized was going to be something special.

Top: Hope begins his career in vaudeville in the 1920s. *Bottom:* Hope in vaudeville, circa 1925.

The Short Subjects

Bob Hope's first venture into movies was a handful of unremarkable short films, the first for Educational Pictures and the next few for the Warner Brothers Vitaphone productions.

Educational and Vitaphone were known for rescuing unfairly forgotten silent screen comics from oblivion. Unfortunately, this was at a time when many of these once-great comedy stars had been ravaged by problems with alcohol, depression, and demon time.

Buster Keaton and Harry Langdon, certainly two of cinema's greatest comic artists, were wasted in cheap Educational productions. While Keaton did have a few diamonds in the rough during this period (*Allez Oop, Grand Slam Opera, One Run Elmer*), none was near the level of his silent films.

Roscoe "Fatty" Arbuckle, who was instrumental in Hope's vaudeville success, returned to films after an eleven-year exile with a series of sound short films produced by Vitaphone. While there were a few laughs in *Hey Pop* and *Buzzin' Around*, again they were pale in comparison to his silents.

However, both studios also used their short films to discover young talent. Sheldon Leonard and Lionel Stander, for instance, both appeared in Vitaphone short films, and their careers lasted well into the television era (Stander survived the McCarthy-era blacklist and Leonard went on to produce *The Andy Griffith Show* and the groundbreaking *I Spy*).

Bob Hope was one of the young, fresh-faced talents that both Educational and Vitaphone felt had potential.

Unfortunately, Hope's talent was not well exhibited at either Educational Pictures the Warner Brothers Vitaphone studio, and today these short films are little more than curiosities.

Hope's inauspicious screen debut was in the Educational Pictures production *Going Spanish* (1934). Directed and co-produced by veteran Al Christie, *Going Spanish* was a typically breezy, yet unremarkable, low-budget comedy.

The plot has Bob, his fiancée (Frances Halliday), and future mother-

Hope in his first film, *Going Spanish* (1934), a two-reel musical comedy also starring Leah Ray.

in-law (Vicki Cummings) passing through the South American town of Los Pochos Eggos. There is a one-day festival during which you can do or say anything to anyone and avoid trouble as long as you sing a song to them afterward. This offbeat premise is used as the basis for a standard boy-girl comedy where both Bob and his girl become interested in other people.

While it does have some measure of historical significance for being his first film, it offers only the most basic outline of the wisecracking character he would assume for most of his film career.

The reception for *Going Spanish* was lukewarm and hardly the sort of thing that spelled future movie stardom for Hope. But *Film Daily*, the only movie-related periodical that regularly reviewed short subjects, liked it, stating:

> Two very promising newcomers to the screen — Bob Hope having scored in the stage hit "Roberta" and Leah Ray well known as a night-club entertainer. Hope is a real comedian, and the girl looks like a sure bet for pictures for she has charm and acting ability as well as good looks.

The movie's shortcomings were not lost on Hope. Running into columnist Walter Winchell, Hope said of *Going Spanish*, "When they catch Dil-
linger they're going to force him to sit through it twice!"

Winchell was amused enough to put Hope's comment in his widely read
newspaper column. Al Christie, however, was not at all amused, and Hope
was not asked to do another film for his company. The comedian soon agreed
to appear in a handful of shorts at Warner Brothers Vitaphone studios.

Hope's first short for Vitaphone was *Paree, Paree* (1934); a two-reel version of Cole Porter's hit Broadway musical "Fifty Million Frenchmen."

While it includes a few songs from the Cole Porter show, allowing Hope
to display the singing voice he had honed on stage, this heavily truncated
version of the musical is little more than a sampler.

It does feature something of a portent to the Hope braggadocio in that
he plays the American who bets his pals he can woo a beautiful woman in
less than thirty days with no money. He gives his friends all of his money
and identification and sets out to win the girl.

Hope comes off well in the role, and his rendition of "You Do Something to Me" is nicely performed. With its succeeding productions, however, it appears rather clear that Vitaphone still didn't quite know how to
utilize his talents.

Film Daily stated:

> Dorothy Stone's dancing, colorful ensemble numbers, and two songs
> by Bob Hope give this Broadway Brevity plenty of entertainment value.
> Hope is a clever comedian but has little opportunity to prove it in this
> picture.

Hope took a break from Vitaphone to emcee a musical variety short
entitled *Soup to Nuts* (1934) for Universal. Although minor, *Film Daily* once
again noticed Hope, stating:

> With Bob Hope as M.C. and an able cast of entertainers, this one
> depicts the Carlton Club as flopping because Allyn Gillyn, wife of Don-
> ald Brian, the owner, won't allow any girl talent owing to her husband's
> propensities in that direction. She gives in, however, and an array of
> talent is trotted forth, including Al Goodman's Orchestra, Vivienne
> Segal, prima donna, Saxon Sisters, singers; Dolores Reade, The Heat
> Waves, Carol & Lane, dancers; and Adrina Otero, a hot Spanish dancer,
> who makes a play for Brian.

Hope was likely recalling his success on the vaudeville stage as a likable, joking master of ceremonies, and it was certainly a precursor to his later
work in radio and television. It should be noted that singer Dolores Reade
became Mrs. Bob Hope.

Returning to Vitaphone later that year, he appeared in a few more shorts during the 1935 to 1936 season, including *Watch the Birdie, The Old Grey Mayor, Double Exposure,* and *Shop Talk,* and *Calling All Tars.* None of these films is particularly distinguishable. In two —*Double Exposure* and *Calling All Tars*—he is teamed with Johnny Berkes in what some have called a primitive harbinger for the type of things he would eventually do with Bing Crosby at Paramount. Actually, Berkes and Hope had none of the chemistry that Hope and Crosby did and appeared to be just what they were — two actors thrown together by the studio in a feeble attempt at creating a comedy team.

The Old Grey Mayor is most typical of Hope's short subjects. Hope is the ne'er-do-well smitten with the mayor's daughter and must outsmart the father in order to succeed in romancing her. It is interesting to see long-time character actor Lionel Stander in support (as the heavy, Hope's chief nemesis), but, as is typical of Vitaphone's Big V comedies, the whole thing seems pretty lackluster.

After completing this handful of short films for Vitaphone in 1935, Hope left motion pictures disillusioned. The past year he had made precious little impact appearing in small-time short films, and he found these to be no stepping stone to more important roles in feature pictures.

Hope stayed off screen for three years, during which he made a hit on Broadway in the musical "Roberta" with George Murphy and Lyda Roberti. However when the musical was filmed by RKO in late 1935, the Hope and Murphy roles were combined and played by Fred Astaire, while Ms. Roberti's part was handled by Ginger Rogers.

Hope did not return to the screen until 1938, but this time in feature films at the prestigious Paramount Pictures.

The Big Broadcast of 1938

Directed by Mitchell Leisen. Story by Frederick Hazlitt Brennan. Story Adapted by Russel Crouse, Howard Lindsay, Walter DeLeon, Ken Englund and Francis Martin. Produced by Harlan Thompson. Original Music by Ralph Rainger, Leo Robin, Tito Guízar, John Leipold and George Parrish. Cinematography by Harry Fischbeck. Photographic Effects by Gordon Jennings. Film Editing by Chandler House and Eda Warren. Art Direction by Hans Dreier and Ernst Fegté. Costume Design by Edith Head. Set Design by A. E. Freudeman. Assistant Director: Edward Anderson. Musical Direction by Boris Morros; Arthur Franklin, advisor. Choreography and Dance Direction by LeRoy Prinz. Sound by Charles Althouse, Don Johnson and Gene Merritt. Animated Sequence Produced by Leon Schlesinger. Presented by Adolph Zukor, President of Paramount Pictures.

Cast: W. C. Fields (T. Frothingill Bellows/S. B. Bellows); Martha Raye (Martha Bellows); Dorothy Lamour (Dorothy Wyndham); Shirley Ross (Cleo Fielding); Lynne Overman (Scoop McPhail): Bob Hope (Buzz Fielding); Ben Blue (Mike); Leif Erikson (Bob Hayes); Patricia Wilder (Honey Chile); Grace Bradley (Grace Fielding); Rufe Davis (Turnkey); Lionel Pape (Lord Harry Droopy); Dorothy Howe (Joan Fielding); Richard Denning (Officer, S.S. Gigantic); Russell Hicks (Capt. Stafford); James Craig (Steward); Archie Twitchell (Steward); Edgar Norton (Bellows' Secretary); Stanley King (Chauffeur); Leonid Kinskey (Ivan); Harry Lauter (Seaman); Wally Maher (Court Clerk Michael Brooke Officer); Don Brodie (Radio Operator); Lorna Gray (Divorcee); Shep Houghton (Bar Patron); Irving Bacon (Prisoner with Harmonica); Jimmy Conlin (First Reporter); Sherry Hall (Second Reporter); James P. Burtis (Third Reporter); Bud Geary (Helmsman); Robert Allen (First Gas Station Man); Jerry Fletcher (Second Gas Station Man); Joe Gray (Sailor); Ray Hanford (Pilot); Carol Adams (Dancer); Muriel Barr (Showgirl); Rebecca Wassem (Haughty Girl); Bernard Punsly, Don Marion, Rex Moore (as caddies); John Hubbard, John Huettner, Clive Morgan, Bill Roberts, Bruce Wyndham (as officers); Kirsten Flagstad, Wilfred Pelletier, Tito Guízar, Shep Fields, Robert Mitchell, Rippling Rhythm Orchestra (as themselves); Monte

Blue, Mary MacLaren, Suzanne Ridgeway, Gertrude Astor, Dorothy Dayton, Paula DeCardo, Yvonne Duval, Nora Gale, Joyce Mathews, Harriette Haddon, Gwen Kenyon, Marion Weldon, Dorothy White, Helaine Moler, Ethel Clayton, Gloria Williams, Nell Craig, Carol Holloway, Florence Wix, Lal Chand Mehra, Harry Wilson, Paul Newlan (bit parts); Estelle Etterre, Mae Busch (extras).

Released February 11, 1938, by Paramount Pictures.

Hope's first feature film appearance was in this mishmash of a movie that survives today mostly due to its eclectic cast.

Review films with music and comedy sketches became popular during the early days of talking pictures, using the new sound technology to its best advantage for the times. The Broadway Melody series at MGM and the Golddiggers series at Warner Brothers often boasted good songs, great dance numbers, and top comic talent.

This Paramount feature should have succeeded in the same manner. The comedy of W. C. Fields, Martha Raye, and Bob Hope, however, was not enough to salvage a film that epitomized the problem of "too many cooks."

What little plot exists in *The Big Broadcast of 1938* deals with a race at sea between two brothers, both played by W. C. Fields. While Fields is able to handily rise to the occasion, the film lets him down.

A truncated version of his golf game, seen to better advantage in earlier Fields films like *The Golf Specialist* (RKO, 1930), *The Dentist* (Paramount, 1932) and *You're Telling Me* (Paramount, 1934), is perhaps the best thing in this picture. The rest of the movie deals primarily with stereotyped characters.

Martha Raye's talents are limited to obtrusive bombast as Fields's wayward daughter. Hope and Shirley Ross play an appropriately breezy romantic couple and are given one great song, "Thanks for the Memory," which was to become Bob's signature tune for the remainder of his career. In fact, the song is the only thing about this movie that was consistently singled out as worthwhile in period reviews.

After sleepwalking through a handful of uneventful short subjects, Bob Hope made his feature film debut inauspiciously, but the strength of the song made him, at the very least, noticeable by the Paramount brass. They realized he was talented enough for pictures. They just weren't quite sure how to use him.

Hope himself has recalled that working on *The Big Broadcast of 1938* was, at the very least, educational. He spent a great deal of time with W. C. Fields and picked the master's brain for ideas about comedy.

Although Fields was drinking heavily throughout the production, it didn't affect his performance. Even back in 1934 when he was making *You're Telling Me* for Paramount, his drinking was a problem for everyone but the drinker. Buster Crabbe, who appeared in *You're Telling Me* told this writer:

"Fields drank all day and never showed it. I don't know how he did it. He almost never forgot his lines, and when he did, he would ad-lib something that was better than what was in the original script."

Hope remembered Fields fondly. When Fields would begin ad-libbing in a ferocious manner, he would look into the camera and drawl, "They're gonna run out of film soon!"

Fields was notoriously suspicious of other performers but took a liking to Hope. In fact, Hope was the only one on the film that was allowed to enter Fields's dressing room.

Hope recalled in a 1993 interview with writer Gary Schneeberger that on one occasion when he was visiting with Fields, there was a knock on the dressing room door. Fields went to the door and was met by a man seeking a charitable contribution. Fields responded by stating that the only charity he ever donated money to was the F.E.B.F. When the man asked what F.E.B.F. stood for, Fields replied, "Fuck Everybody But Fields."

College Swing

Directed by Raoul Walsh. Assistant Director Roland Asher. Writing credits: Frederick Hazlitt Brennan, Walter DeLeon, Francis Martin, Preston Sturges. Story Idea by Ted Lesser. Produced by Lewis E. Gensler. Presented by Adolph Zukor. Songs by Hoagy Carmichael, Burton Lane, Frank Loesser and Manning Sherwin. Incidental Music by Gordon Jenkins, John Leipold, Victor Young. Music Advisor: Arthur Franklin. Music Director: Boris Morros. Dance Director: Leroy Prinz. Cinematography by Victor Milner. Film Editing by Leroy Stone. Art Direction by Hans Dreier and Ernst Fegté. Costume Design by Edith Head. Makeup by Wally Westmore. Set Decorations by A. E. Freudeman. Sound by Harold Lewis and Howard Wilson.

Cast: George Burns (George Jonas); Gracie Allen (Gracie Alden); Martha Raye (Mabel); Bob Hope (Bud Brady); Edward Everett Horton (Hubert Dash); Florence George (Ginna Ashburn); Ben Blue (Ben Volt); Betty Grable (Betty); Jackie Coogan (Jackie); John Payne (Martin Bates); Cecil Cunningham (Dean Sleet); Tully Marshall (Grandpa Alden); Robert Cummings (Radio Announcer); Skinnay Ennis (Skinnay); Barlowe Borland (Dean); Jerry Colonna (Prof. Yascha Koloski); Jerry Bergen (Prof. Jasper Chinn); Edward LeSaint (Dr. Storm); Charles Trowbridge (Dr. Ashburn); Richard Denning (Student); John Hubbard (Student); Dorothy White (Dancer); Mary Livingstone (Usherette); Alphonse Martell (Headwaiter); Irving Bacon, June Ray, Jack Slate (bit parts); Bob Mitchell and St. Brendan's Choristers (themselves).

Released April 29, 1938, by Paramount Pictures.

Another breezy musical produced by Paramount's B unit, *College Swing* only retains some interest today for its cast.

As with most musicals of this sort, the plot is threadbare.

What little plot there is belongs to Gracie Allen. Allen and husband George Burns made up a successful comedy team that scored a big hit on radio, a minor hit in films, and another major hit years later on television. Gracie played the ditzy counterpart to Burns's bewildered straight man. Her special brand of airheaded logic was amusing enough to remain popular from the duo's vaudeville beginnings well into the TV age.

In this movie, Gracie is trying to graduate from college, but her lack of logic and understanding is holding her back. This minor plot serves as the basis for appearances by several top radio stars.

Bob Hope's contribution is easily lost in the shuffle, although he did secure a reasonably larger part than some of the other players, mostly due to producer Lewis Gensler. Gensler was duly impressed with Hope's breezy style in *The Big Broadcast of 1938* and thus gave him a fairly good supporting role in this feature. However, the fact that this is little more than another musical review indicates that Hope did nothing more than he had already done in *The Big Broadcast of 1938*.

Perhaps the most interesting aspect of this film was the chance to see a lot of old vaudeville performers do some of their specialty numbers. Gracie Allen, for instance, started out dancing Irish jigs on stage as a small child. Here she performs her old vaudeville dance, much in the same way she had done in an act with her sisters two decades earlier.

Florence George, in her first of only two films, does the song "Moments Like This," which is the only good song in the movie. She has the romantic lead opposite a young John Payne. Payne would later have a solid career in 20th Century Fox musicals before settling into predominantly westerns toward the end of his career.

Betty Grable was only twenty-one years old when she did this picture but had already appeared in over forty films. Only a few short years before becoming a favorite GI pinup, Grable did several dance numbers, most notably with her then husband Jackie Coogan.

Coogan had been a child star in silent pictures like *My Boy* and Charlie Chaplin's classic *The Kid*. As with many child actors, he had trouble maintaining a solid foothold on film stardom as he aged. Hope has recalled that when Coogan guested on Hope's radio show, they did a bit about his child star status. Coogan stated that he ruined his own career. When Hope asked how, Coogan replied, "I grew up!" There was a subtext that wasn't very funny. Of course Coogan did manage to remain active to the end of his life, even to the point of becoming a household name to a new generation via television as Uncle Fester on *The Addams Family* from 1965 to 1967.

Edward Everett Horton, a veteran character actor who also did radio, is especially amusing in his sequences with Gracie Allen, trying to sort out her peculiar brand of illogical logic. Hope once recalled that Horton was notoriously frugal, despite being a well-paid character performer for most of his life. Once, when a sixtyish Horton showed up to rehearse for a radio show, he was wearing his old letter sweater from college!

Hope has written that at this point he was considering leaving movies for good. He did two review pictures, made very marginal impact, and didn't appear to have much else to offer. Instead he stuck it out and tried to think of a way to graduate from Paramount's B-picture unit to the more prestigious A pictures.

Give Me a Sailor

Directed by Elliott Nugent. Written by Doris Anderson and Frank Butler. From the play by Anne Nichols. Produced by Harold Hurley, Jeff Lazarus (producers) and Paul Jones (associate producer). Cinematography by Victor Milner. Film Editing by William Shea. Art Direction by Hans Dreier and A. Earl Hedrick. Songs by Ralph Rainger and Leo Robin. Incidental Music by John Leipold and David Rose. Musical Direction by Boris Morros. Choreography by LeRoy Prinz.

Cast: Martha Raye (Letty Larkin); Bob Hope (Jim Brewster); Betty Grable (Nancy Larkin); Jack Whiting (Walter Brewster); Clarence Kolb (Captain Tallant); J. C. Nugent (Mr. Larkin); Bonnie Jean Churchill (Ethel May Brewster); Nana Bryant (Mrs. Brewster); Kathleen Lockhart (Mrs. Hawks); Emerson Treacy (Meryl); Ralph Sanford (Ice Man); Edward Earle (1st Businessman); Eddie Kane (2nd Businessman); Eddie Borden (bit part).

Released August 19, 1938, by Paramount Pictures.

The Paramount brass apparently felt Bob Hope worked well with Martha Raye because they are teamed for the third time in Hope's third picture for the studio.

This time, however, the two comics are not caught up in a musical review. They are the co-stars of a comedy feature that appears to be tailored to their respective talents.

Hope plays Jim Brewster, a navy man as is his brother, Walter. Both have been interested in pretty Nancy Larkin (Betty Grable) since they were youngsters. Nancy's ugly duckling sister Letty (Martha Raye) likes Walter, so she and Jim have been plotting so that Jim will eventually end up with Nancy and Letty will get Walter. The plot, which has been going on since they were children, even has its own code, complete with code book. Of course the ending is predictable — trusted friends Jim and Letty end up together.

Despite the standard B-picture plot, *Give Me a Sailor* is fast moving

Bob Hope, Nana Bryant, J. C. Nugent, Martha Raye (on couch), Betty Grable and Bonnie Jean Churchill (left to right) in *Give Me a Sailor* (1938).

and a lot of fun. Raye, given top billing above the title, is showcased in fine fashion. Sometimes her sad scenes are a little much, but her comedy sequences are a delight, with her characteristic exuberance and lack of inhibition.

Hope is given second billing, also above the title, which shows that Paramount was indeed aware of his talents. However, while Hope turns in another typically breezy performance, he was already longing to find his way out of the B-picture doldrums and become cast in more prestigious A pictures.

Hope's double-take style is on display in *Give Me a Sailor*. Rather than rely on the physical double-take that had been a staple of comedy movies since silent pictures, Hope also used his voice. For instance, when Letty is slated to attend a picnic with Walter, she suddenly overhears that he plans to ditch her and sneak off with Nancy. She locks herself in her room and cries. Jim, arriving to escort Letty to the picnic and sneak off with Nancy himself, calls to her from outside her room. She states that she has decided not to go. Hope, as Jim, reacts not only with a physical double-take but he also reacts verbally:

> "Yeah, you get ready and (pause — double-take) Hey, wait a minute, whaddya mean you aren't going?!"

This style became something of a trait for Hope. On radio he had to, essentially, double-take verbally in this fashion. On film, he can combine verbal and physical to perform a most artful, creative double-take that was perfectly suited for the changing style of screen comedy.

By 1939, comedy movies were changing. The silent screen comedians who managed to make the transition to talking pictures were already waning. Laurel and Hardy were about to end their long-time association with Roach and sign with 20th Century Fox, altering their act for the times with results that were not always successful. Buster Keaton was bumbling through a series of weak shorts at Columbia, as was Harry Langdon. Chaplin was not to enter the talking picture revolution for another year. Harold Lloyd had made *Professor Beware* the year before and then entered a hiatus that lasted nearly a decade.

The new comic breed, coming from vaudeville, burlesque, and radio, relied on smart patter, quips, and witty repartee. Verbal timing was as important as physical timing. Hope, breezily pleasant and funny, seemed a perfect fit for this era. Paramount certainly recognized this but still wasn't quite sure how they should use him.

This is not to claim that *Give Me a Sailor* completely eschews physical comedy. In one of the film's highlights, Letty overuses a powerful facial cream, which hardens into a cement-like substance on her face. Hope must punch her to break it off. Period reviews pointed out this routine as eliciting gales of laughter from the audience.

Give Me a Sailor is, decidedly, more a Raye picture than a Hope picture. Bob is clearly in support. His performance, however, while not yet honed, contains many of the elements of the character that would soon become one of the most beloved in all of filmdom. *Give Me a Sailor* shows Hope in transition. The breezy, personable character he had played in the earlier short subjects a few years before now has more depth of personality. His comedy comes as much from his performance as from the film's situations. In his next few pictures, Hope perfected this style.

Thanks for the Memory

Directed by George Archainbaud. Written by Lynn Starling. From the play "Up Pops the Devil" by Albert Hackett and Frances Goodrich. Produced by Mel Shauer. Cinematography by Karl Struss. Film Editing by Alma Macrorie. Art Direction by Franz Bachelin and Hans Dreier. Original Music by Hoagy Carmichael and Frank Loesser, Ralph Rainger and Leo Robin. Musical Director: Boris Morros.

Cast: Bob Hope (Steve Merrick); Shirley Ross (Anne Merrick); Charles Butterworth (Biney); Otto Kruger (Gil Morrell); Hedda Hopper (Polly Griscom); Laura Hope Crews (Mrs. Kent); Emma Dunn (Mrs. Platt); Roscoe Karns (George Kent); Eddie "Rochester" Anderson (Janitor); Edward Gargan (Flanahan); Jack Norton (Bert Monroe); Patricia Wilder (Luella); William Collier, Sr. (Mr. Platt); Barney Dean (Kelly); Pat West (Refuse Man); June Brewster (Frances); Mary Brodel (Clara); Jack Chapin (Messenger); Vernon Dent (Refuse Man); Tom Dugan (Taxi Driver); Lillian Herlein (Landlady); Johnny Morris (Newsboy); Luana Walters (Model); Sheila Darcy (Model); Gwen Kenyon (Model).

Released November 11, 1938.

While Hope was filming his second and third pictures, the song "Thanks for the Memory" that he and Shirley Ross had introduced in *The Big Broadcast of 1938* became an enormous hit. Paramount got the idea to team Hope and Ross in a seriocomic domestic feature in order to capitalize on the song.

Thanks for the Memory is one of Hope's least-seen pictures. It is, at the very least, interesting on a few levels.

First, Hope and Ross are not appearing as the same sort of couple Hope and Raye were in *Give Me a Sailor*. Rather, Hope and Ross are an example of post–Depression, pre-war domesticity, using the situations for humor and drama.

Hope would, many years later, team with Lucille Ball for a similar domestic comedy-drama, *The Facts of Life* (1960). While *Thanks for the Memory* is really not a precursor, it still represents an early example of Hope doing

Hope with Shirley Ross in *The Big Broadcast of 1938*.

a type of picture that he would perform most effectively after having solidified his legendary status.

Paramount's intention was likely to experiment with Hope. Perhaps they felt Hope could carry a series of B-level romantic comedy-dramas in which he could utilize the breezy style for which he had already become noted and still maintain a domestic drama that could be appealing and comfortable in the second half of a double bill.

Hope, interested in being elevated to A pictures, likely took the job to prove his versatility as an actor, drawing from some of the training he'd had on Broadway.

Hope plays Steve Merrick, a writer working on a novel. Like most writers he procrastinates more than he writes. His penchant for partying and avoiding the work at hand becomes a sore point in his marriage to Anne (Shirley Ross). Money becomes tight, and Anne wants to go to work, but Steve's pride won't allow his wife to enter the workforce, despite the very real need for more income.

The musical highlight, other than a rehash of the title song, is "Two Sleepy People," which also became a hit, but not nearly as big a hit as "Thanks for the Memory."

Never Say Die

Directed by Elliott Nugent. Assistant Director: Harold Schwartz. Written by Frank Butler, Don Hartman and Preston Sturges. From the play by William H. Post. Produced by Paul Jones. Cinematography by Leo Tover. Film Editing by James Smith. Art Direction by Hans Dreier and Ernst Fegté. Costume Design by Edith Head. Makeup by Wally Westmore. Set Design by A. E. Freudeman. Songs by Ralph Rainger, Leo Robin, Charles Bradshaw and John Leipold. Incidental Music by Milan Roder and Leo Shuken. Sound Recordists: Walter Oberst and Philip Wisdom. Photographic Effects by Farciot Edouart.

Cast: Martha Raye (Mickey Hawkins); Bob Hope (John Kidley); Andy Devine (Henry Munch); Alan Mowbray (Prince Smirnov); Gale Sondergaard (Juno Marko); Sig Ruman (Poppa Ingleborg); Ernest Cossart (Jeepers); Paul Harvey (Jasper Hawkins); Frances Arms (Momma Ingleborg); Monty Woolley (Dr. Schmidt); Ivan F. Simpson (Kretsky [as Ivan Simpson]); Albert Dekker (Kidley's Second); Foy Van Dolsen (Kretsky's Bodyguard); Donald Haines (Julius); Christian Rub (The Mayor); Hobart Cavanaugh (Druggist); Victor Kilian (Man Who Loads Pistols); Frank Reicher (Man in Charge of Duel); Gustav Von Seyffertitz (Chemist); Hans Conried and Gino Corrado (bit parts).

Released April 14, 1939, by Paramount Pictures.

The Raye-Hope partnership once again is cast in a fast-paced, enjoyable comedy, their fourth and last film together.

Hope plays John Kidley, a man who believes he has two months to live. While visiting a Swiss spa, he saves a girl, Mickey (Martha Raye), from suicide and hastily decides to marry her. They barely know each other, of course, and are smitten with others, but they shrug all of this off and forge ahead.

Of course the film is predictable: John wants out of the marriage once he realizes he is not dying, and the couple does end up falling for each other just as they eventually did in *Give Me a Sailor*.

Preston Sturges is credited as one of the screenwriters, which may account for some of the more amusing moments, including a duel scene that features some tongue-twisting dialog. When Hope does the bit where he must remember that there's a cross on the muzzle of the pistol with the bullet and a nick on the handle of the pistol with the blank, it immediately recalls similar sequences in his 1948 film *The Paleface* in which he must remember several directions to succeed in the duel (he shoots with his left, so lean to your right, etc.). It also recalls the "chalice in the palace" routine done by Danny Kaye in *The Court Jester*.

Still in all, *Never Say Die* is merely an amusing, trivial production that still indicates that Paramount's interest in Hope was for him to headline B pictures. The fact that he is again opposite Raye leads one to assume a teaming was considered. However, since this is their last film together, it is likely that Paramount realized Hope's star power in time for him to finally graduate to A pictures. Unfortunately, this was not evident by his next picture.

Some Like It Hot

Directed by George Archainbaud. Written by Lewis R. Foster and Wilkie C. Mahoney. From the play "The Great Magoo" by Ben Hecht and Gene Fowler. Produced by William C. Thomas, associate producer. Cinematography by Karl Struss. Film Editing by Edward Dmytryk. Art Direction by Hans Dreier and A. Earl Hedrick. Sound by George Dutton and Walter Oberst. Musical Advisor: Arthur Franklin.

Cast: Bob Hope (Nicky Nelson); Shirley Ross (Lily Racquet); Una Merkel (Flo Saunders); Gene Krupa (himself); Rufe Davis (Stoney); Bernard Nedell (Stephen Hanratty); Frank Sully (Sailor Burke); Bernadene Hayes (Miss Marble); Richard Denning (Mr. Weems); Jack Smart (Joe); Pat West (Flo's Partner); Harry Barris (Harry, Piano Player); Nora Cecil (Mrs. Beckett); Clarence Wilson (Mr. Ives); Jack Chapin (Cook); Dudley Dickerson (Sam); Byron Foulger (Radio Announcer); Edgar Dearing (MacCrady); Wayne "Tiny" Whitt (Bass Fiddler); Eddie Kane (Man in Waiting Room); Tempe Pigott (Flower Woman); Russ Powell (Pancake Man).

Released May 19, 1939, by Paramount Pictures.

Hope often cited *Some Like It Hot* as his worst film from this period of his career, and deservedly so.

This time Hope is Nicky, a sideshow owner who uses the wealthy Lili (Shirley Ross) to raise money for the show. There is some good period music, but the film's status as a throwaway is terribly evident.

Hope's other features up to this point were B pictures as well, but they were the type of solid, entertaining B pictures that larger studios like Paramount would produce as second-feature entries for double bills. These films were tight, entertaining warm-ups that led into the more prestigious headline movies. At their best, they are most entertaining.

While films like *Give Me a Sailor* and *Never Say Die* are the sort of entertaining movies that represent a B-picture unit at its best, a film like *Some Like It Hot* is little more than a cheesy attempt to capitalize on the budding popularity of swing music.

Perhaps it was felt that the breezy style Hope had established would play well to a film that was essentially directed toward a teen audience. However, as Hope stated in his book *The Road to Hollywood*, after *Some Like It Hot* there was no way to go but up.

Fortunately, his next picture proved to be a stepping stone toward the A list.

This was to be Hope's last appearance with Shirley Ross. She made a few more films, but real stardom eluded her. After her career faded out, she became reclusive. When she died in 1975, even Hope had no idea of her whereabouts.

Another film entitled *Some Like It Hot* was made by Billy Wilder in 1959. It has been named by the American Film Institute as the greatest comedy feature in movie history. It has nothing to do with this forgettable Bob Hope entry.

The Hope film has often been retitled *Rhythm Romance* on television.

The Cat and the Canary

Directed by Elliott Nugent. Writing by Walter DeLeon and Lynn Starling. From the play by John Willard. Produced by Arthur Hornblow, Jr. Cinematography by Charles Lang. Film Editing by Archie Marshek. Art Direction by Hans Dreier and Robert Usher. Set Decoration by A. E. Freudeman. Costume Design by Edith Head. Original Music by Ernst Toch. Musical Advisor: Andrea Setaro. Sound Recordists: Richard Olson and Philip Wisdom.

Cast: Bob Hope (Wally Campbell); Paulette Goddard (Joyce Norman); John Beal (Fred Blythe); Douglass Montgomery (Charles Wilder); Gale Sondergaard (Miss Lu); Elizabeth Patterson (Aunt Susan); George Zucco (Lawyer Crosby); Nydia Westman (Cicily); John Wray (Hendricks); George Regas (Indian Guide); Milton Kibbee (Photographer); Charles Lane (Reporter); Frank Melton (Reporter); Chief Thundercloud (Indian Guide).

Released November 10, 1939, by Paramount Pictures.

A comical remake of Paul Leni's classic silent film, *The Cat and the Canary* utilizes all of the rudimentary haunted house bits that had been established in earlier movies, especially its pioneering predecessor.

A group of six relatives goes to a creepy house for a will reading. Joyce (Paulette Goddard) is the sole heir, but a second will has been made in case Joyce has fallen victim to the insanity that runs in the family. This puts Joyce in danger. The maid (Gale Sondergaard) warns that the spirits have indicated that one of them will die that night. Shortly thereafter, word arrives that a mad killer has escaped from the local insane asylum.

All of the ingredients are here: an inheritance, a group of relatives and others close to the deceased, unexplained events, murders, and a twist ending. Actors particularly adept at appearing as mysterious characters, such as George Zucco and Gale Sondargaard, help add authenticity.

In the context of Hope's film career, *The Cat and the Canary* is significant as the film that helped solidify his movie stardom and eventually propel him to the A-picture status he'd coveted.

27

Hope shields Paulette Goddard from Gale Sondergaard's piercing stare in *The Cat and the Canary* (1939).

Hope's character, however, was little different from his previous films. He was once again the breezy wiseacre. His comic style was amusing, but it was not the sort that would presumably cause film executives to take notice.

However, by the time of *The Cat and the Canary*, Hope had established himself as a star on radio. His rat-a-tat delivery and quips were perfect for the household medium, and American audiences tuned in regularly to hear him play opposite guest stars whose film careers were on a decidedly higher plane. Thus, despite that it was really no better than the pleasantly amusing *Give Me a Sailor* or *Never Say Die*, *The Cat and the Canary* was a huge box office success. Fans of Hope's radio program, coupled with moviegoers who had enjoyed him in his other films, all flocked to see his latest picture. It is another solid B movie, but one that generated A-picture box office results.

It was generally believed among writers who worked primarily in B pictures and short subjects of the period that the best way to get surefire audience reaction is to place comedians in the context of a horror picture. Scares and laughs blend nicely together if good material is available. *The Cat and the Canary* is an established haunted house story; in fact, it is a remake of what is considered the pioneer of this style. While Hope does indeed add a comic touch, the film is essentially a haunted house mystery rather than a comedy.

Paulette Goddard was dating Charlie Chaplin at the time she was filming *The Cat and the Canary*. At a social event, Chaplin approached Hope and complimented him on his sense of timing. Hope, who'd revered Chaplin since childhood, recalled that moment as a tremendous inspiration.

The popularity of *The Cat and the Canary* gave Hope a stronger foothold on his film career. Because of his association through radio with a couple of Paramount's top stars, his next picture would be of the A status he craved.

Road to Singapore

Directed by Victor Schertzinger. Assistant Director George Templeton. Writing Credits: Frank Butler, Barney Dean, Ray Golden and Don Hartman. From a story by Harry Hervey. Special Sequences Written by Ray Golden and Sid Kuller. Esperanto Language Textual Material by Joseph Scherer. Produced by Harlan Thompson. Executive Producer: William LeBaron. Cinematography by William C. Mellor. Film Editing by Paul Weatherwax. Art Direction by Hans Dreier and Robert Odell. Costume Design by Edith Head. Art Department: A. E. Freudeman (interior decorator). Songs by Johnny Burke and James V. Monaco ("Too Romantic," "Sweet Potato Piper," and "Kaigoon") and Victor Schertzinger ("The Moon and the Willow" and "Captain Custard"). Incidental Music by Victor Young. Sound Recordists: John Cope, Earl Hayman. Musical Direction by Victor Young. Choreography by Leroy Prinz.

Cast: Bing Crosby (Josh Mallon); Dorothy Lamour (Mima); Bob Hope (Ace Lannigan); Charles Coburn (Joshua Mallon IV); Judith Barrett (Gloria Wycott); Steve Pendleton (Gordon Wycot); Anthony Quinn (Caesar); Jerry Colonna (Achilles Bombanassa); Pierre Watkin (Morgan Wycott); Miles Mander (Sir Malcolm Drake); Gloria Franklin (Ninky Poo); Johnny Arthur (Timothy Willow); Roger Gray (Cherry's Father); Harry Bradley (Secretary); Don Brodie (Fred); Arthur Q. Bryan (Bartender); Elvia Allman (Homely Girl); Edward Gargan (Bill); Greta Granstedt (Babe); Grace Hayle (Chaperone on Yacht); Edmund Mortimer (Chaperone's Companion); Monte Blue (High Priest); Robert Emmett O'Connor (Immigration Officer); Marguerita Padula (Proprietress); Jack Pepper (Newspaper Columnist); John Kelly (Sailor); Kitty Kelly (Sailor's Wife); Richard Keene (Cameraman); Pedro Regas (Zato, a Policeman); Robert St. Angelo (Native Policeman); Fred Malatesta (Native Policeman); Belle Mitchell (Native Shopkeeper); Richard Tucker (Officer on Ship); Cyril Ring (Ship's Officer); Claire James (Girl at Party); Helen Lynd (Society Girl); Carmen D'Antonio (Native Girl); Paula DeCardo (Native Dancing Girl); Benny Inocencio (Native Boy); Fred Walburn (Boy); Payne B. Johnson (Boy); Bobby Barber (Man Hit with Soap Suds); Henry Norris (Shipboard Extra).

Released March 22, 1940, by Paramount Pictures.

Bob Hope received third billing, after Bing Crosby and Dorothy Lamour, in what can be considered his first A picture, *Road to Singapore.*

The other featured players had already been established. Crosby was a major singing star and long-time Paramount actor, already having appeared in *Mississippi* (1935) opposite W. C. Fields as well as in several popular Paramount musicals.

Dorothy Lamour had made a sensation in *The Hurricane* (1937). Her tantalizing appearance made her commonly known as *The Sarong Girl* for most of her career.

Hope was, at this point, perceived as a competent B-picture comedian with a radio show that was gaining popularity.

This film was originally titled *The Road to Mandalay* and was slated to star Fred MacMurray and Jack Oakie. When both actors passed on the script, it was given to Crosby, George Burns, and Gracie Allen. Crosby liked it, but Burns and Allen passed. The project was then shelved.

Dorothy Lamour recalls having lunch with Crosby and Hope in the studio commissary and being unable to eat due to laughing so hard. Crosby and Hope would naturally segue into wordplay and comic quips so effortlessly, it always amused those around them. Word got around, and when a film project was needed for Crosby, the old *Road to Mandalay* script was dusted off, Hope was hired, and Lamour was brought on board as well. The locale changed to Singapore to capitalize on Lamour's Sarong Girl status.

What is most interesting about this first Road picture is how different Hope's character is from ensuing releases. While in the forthcoming Road films he is cowardly and easily duped by Crosby, in this first entry he is a brash iconoclast who is outwardly quite sure of himself. While the superficial brashness would remain a part of his character, it was later used to mask his cowardly insecurities. This element would bolster his appeal with audiences in much the same manner that pathos added depth to the character of many silent screen comedians.

Of course when one considers the difference in Hope's character from this first Road picture to the next, one must take into account that Paramount had no plans to turn this into a series. In fact, they figured *Road to Singapore* would be little more than a pleasant diversion. They underestimated its box office potential. *Road to Singapore* turned out to be a tremendous hit. It was not only Hope's most successful film to date but Crosby's and Lamour's as well.

The plot deals with playboy Bing's impending nuptials to a society girl (Judith Barrett). His father, a shipping mogul (Charles Coburn), wants Bing

Hope, Dorothy Lamour and Bing Crosby (left to right) in *Road to Singapore* (1940).

to settle down and join the business. However, he is far more attracted to Hope's carefree single life and flees the marriage. They hide out in Singapore and meet sarong-clad Lamour, who is part of a dangerous vaudeville act where cigarettes are snapped out of her mouth by a bullwhip. They help her escape from her partner (Anthony Quinn).

Some of the elements that became staples in the ensuing Road pictures are established in this first entry. Both Crosby and Hope vie for the attention of Lamour, but unlike later films, the rivalry seems to be more relaxed and equal. There is no real evidence of Crosby putting one over on Hope. In fact, when Lamour initially chooses Hope over Crosby, Bing is understanding. "He'll spend all your money and never make a quarter. But he'll hand you a million laughs."

In the end, when Lamour admits she really wanted Crosby all along but didn't want to come between him and Barrett, Hope is equally understanding. "She's wanted you all along, you fool," he states good-naturedly. All are happy at the end.

Crosby getting the girl became something of a running gag in the eventual Road series. It even bled into other Hope vehicles in which Crosby did not co-star, and it was occasional fodder on Hope's radio program.

In an interview with writer Gary Schneeberger, Hope quipped, "I got the girl in most of my pictures, but in the Road films I gave in to the older fella."

In retrospect, *Road to Singapore* is generally regarded as one of the weaker entries in the Road series. However, *New Yorker* critic Pauline Kael recognized it as still an amusing entertainment in her book *5001 Nights at the Movies*:

> Bob Hope and Bing Crosby sauntering along, singing and appearing as innocent, practical jokes, while Dorothy Lamour keeps house for them on a South Sea island. She wears an expression of intense domesticity, a trim sarong, and a hibiscus; a frown of chaste speculation darkens her brow when she must decide which of these two nice boys she will specifically love, honor and obey. In spite of this problem of sentiment, it's a happy, unpretentious farce.

The success of *Road to Singapore* upon its initial release benefited Hope's career tremendously. Along with establishing him as a major film attraction, it strengthened the popularity of his radio program. Furthermore, Hope was asked to emcee the 1940 Academy Awards ceremonies, honoring the films of 1939. It was a job he would maintain for many decades.

Hope was on the road to superstardom.

The Ghost Breakers

Directed by George Marshall. Writing by Walter DeLeon. Based on the play by Paul Dickey and Charles W. Goddard. Produced by Arthur Hornblow, Jr. Cinematography by Charles Lang. Film Editing by Ellsworth Hoagland. Art Direction by Hans Dreier and Robert Usher. Costume Design by Edith Head. Set Decoration by A. E. Freudeman. Original Music by Ernst Toch and Victor Young. Sound Recordists: Harold Lewis and Richard Olson.

Cast: Bob Hope (Larry Lawrence); Paulette Goddard (Mary Carter); Richard Carlson (Geoff Montgomery); Paul Lukas (Parada); Willie Best (Alex); Pedro de Cordoba (Havez); Virginia Brissac (Mother Zombie); Noble Johnson (The Zombie); Anthony Quinn (Ramon/Francisco Mederos); Tom Dugan (Raspy Kelly); Paul Fix (Frenchy Duval); Lloyd Corrigan (Martin); Blanca Vischer (Dolores); James Blaine (Police Sergeant); Herbert Elliott (Lt. Murray); Douglas Kennedy (Intern); Francisco Marán (Headwaiter); James Flavin (Hotel Porter); David Durand (Bellhop); Jack Edwards (Ship Bellboy); Leonard Sues (Newsboy); Paul Newlan (Newsboy); Max Wagner (Ship Porter); Jack Hatfield (Elevator Boy); Jack Norton (Drunk); Robert Ryan (Intern); Kay Stewart (Telephone Girl); Grace Hayle (Screaming Woman); Emmett Vogan (Announcer).

Released June 21, 1940, by Paramount Pictures.

When *The Ghost Breakers* was first chosen by the Paramount brass as an upcoming Hope vehicle, he was still working on *Road to Singapore.* They didn't realize what a hit the first Road picture would be and still weren't quite sure how to market this brash, popular radio personality. Hence, the conventional wisdom was to place Hope in the same context as his biggest hit, which up to that time was *The Cat and the Canary,* and see if lightning would strike twice.

That is, perhaps, the interesting problem with Hope's films during this period. Initially placed into a series of B pictures in order to see where he'd fit in, Paramount often experimented by using formulas that had worked before.

After Hope debuted in *The Big Broadcast of 1938*, Paramount gave him another light musical review, *College Swing*. After some chemistry with Martha Raye was evident in *Give Me a Sailor*, Hope was paired with her again in the similar *Never Say Die*. When his duet with Shirley Ross in *The Big Broadcast of 1938* became a hit, Paramount teamed the two of them up in a musical titled the same as the hit song, *Thanks for the Memory*.

Now the success of *The Cat and the Canary* yielded *The Ghost Breakers*, once again with his co-star from *Canary*, Paulette Goddard. Fortunately, it is an improvement over the first and maintained Hope's rising box office popularity.

Hope plays Larry Lawrence, a radio personality who specializes in gossip, especially gossip that concerns local mobsters.

One of Larry's listeners, Mary Carter (Paulette Goddard), discovers she's inherited an island off the Cuban Coast. Despite rumors that the island is haunted, Mary is undaunted.

Larry's gossip program annoys local gangsters, who summon him to their hotel. He arrives, believes himself to be in hot water, and borrows a gun from his manservant Alex (Willie Best). When a homicide occurs, Larry believes that he accidentally has killed the man. While fleeing police, he finds himself in Mary's room and hides in her trunk. The trunk is thrown onto the ship that is taking Mary to her island, so Larry ends up going along. Once they arrive on the island, it is obvious that they are not alone.

While quite similar in structure to *The Cat and the Canary*, *The Ghost Breakers* is, nevertheless, an amusing comedy and helped Hope's status in movies to rise. The script is filled with smart quips. Upon first barging into Mary's room, Lawrence warns, "Don't scream. If there's going to be any hysterics, I'll have them." When en route to the island he is told that it is infested with zombies "who have deadened eyes and do things without any idea as to what they are doing." "You mean like Democrats?" Lawrence asks.

Perhaps the most interesting thing about Hope's performance in *The Ghost Breakers* is that his character is really not a coward. While he makes quips about being frightened, Lawrence is rather heroically protective of Mary. When a bucket of sand is dropped from above and narrowly misses them, Lawrence goes after the culprit. When he is told of the island being haunted, he slyly remarks, "You know what I'd do if I saw a ghost? I'd take a shot at him." This is far different from the phony bravado exhibited by the cowardly characters Hope plays in other films.

Paulette Goddard offers a performance that works beyond her limitations as an ingénue. She is fully a co-star and there are scenes featuring her in which Hope does not appear at all. As with any of her screen appearances, she handles the action and supporting drama effectively.

Many welcome veterans appear in supporting roles, with a young Anthony Quinn a standout as twins (one of whom is murdered early on), Lloyd Corrigan as an amusingly intrusive red herring, and a short bit in which classic movie drunk Jack Norton sees Lawrence speaking to his manservant from inside the trunk and believes the servant to be a brilliant ventriloquist. This bit was redone with Frank Fontaine in *Scared Stiff*, a 1953 remake with Dean Martin and Jerry Lewis.

Willie Best, a black comedian whose outrageous reactions in horror sequences relegated him to appearing as a stereotype for most of his career, does a nice job working past his stereotypical limitations and is one of the most enjoyable things in the film. Best maintained a steady, lucrative career well into the television era until he died of cancer while still in his forties.

The tremendous box office success of *The Ghost Breakers* helped Paramount to realize that Bob Hope had become a bona fide movie star. It remains one of the best films from the earlier part of his screen career.

Road to Zanzibar

Directed by Victor Schertzinger. Assistant Director: Hal Walker. Written by Frank Butler and Don Hartman. Based on the story "Find Colonel Fawcett" by Don Hartman and Sy Bartlett. Special Gags by Barney Dean. Produced by Paul Jones. Executive Producer: William LeBaron. Cinematography by Ted Tetzlaff. Film Editing by Alma Macrorie. Art Direction by Hans Dreier and Robert Usher. Costume Design by Edith Head. Makeup by Wally Westmore and Harry Ray. Sound Recordists: Earl Hayman and Don Johnson. Original Music by Jimmy Van Heusen and Johnny Burke. Choreography by LeRoy Prinz.

Cast: Bing Crosby (Chuck Reardon); Bob Hope (Hubert "Fearless" Frazier); Dorothy Lamour (Donna Latour); Una Merkel (Julia Quimby); Eric Blore (Charles Kimble); Norma Varden (Clara Kimble); Douglass Dumbrille (Slave Trader); Lionel Royce (Monsieur Lebec); Buck Woods (Thonga); Leigh Whipper (Scarface); Ernest Whitman (Whiteface); Noble Johnson (Chief); Joan Marsh (Dimples, Helper in Human Cannonball Act); Luis Alberni (Native Booth Proprietor); Robert Middlemass (Police Inspector); Al Bridge Colonial (Policeman with Inspector); Iris Adrian (French Soubrette in Cafe); James B. Carson (Waiter with Champagne); Eddie Conrad (Barber); Richard Keene (Clerk); Georges Renavent (Saunders, Hotel Owner); Henry Roquemore (Cafe Proprietor); Jules Strongbow (Solomon); Leo Gorcey (Boy); Paul Porcasi (Turk at Slave Market); Ethel Loreen Greer (Fat Lady); Charles Gemora (Gorilla); Harry C. Johnson (Acrobat); Harry Johnson, Jr. (Acrobat); Laverne Vess (Curzon Sister — Iron Jaw Act); Priscilla White (Curzon Sister — Iron Jaw Act); Ken Carpenter (Commentator [Voice]).

Released April 11, 1941, by Paramount Pictures.

Road to Zanzibar is the second in the Road series and one of the weaker entries overall. However, it is interesting for a variety of reasons.

First, the Hope character most familiar in the Road pictures establishes itself here, including his cowardliness and being a patsy for the wily Crosby. Second, it makes references to the previous film (including a version of the pat-a-cake bit, which they allude to as having become popular). Finally, it maintains the basic premise of Hope and Crosby helping Lamour out of a perilous situation.

Chuck Reardon (Crosby) and his pal Fearless Frazier (Hope) flee a South African carnival when their sideshow act goes awry and causes a fire that burns the show to the ground. They've finally saved enough to return to New York when Chuck invests it all in a lost diamond mine. A pair of attractive con-women soon trick the boys into financing a safari.

From this point the gags are generally rather ordinary. Old jungle picture wheezes like cannibals planning to eat Hope and Crosby and later being duped into thinking they are gods are only mildly amusing.

One highlight features Hope in a wrestling match with a gorilla (played by long-time ape imitator Charles Gemora). Another features Hope and Crosby doing their pat-a-cake bit, which delights the horde of natives as they erupt into a violent game themselves, allowing the boys to escape.

Road to Zanzibar began life in script form as a drama entitled *Find Colonel Fawcett*. It was reworked by comedy writers Frank Butler and Don Hartman (who co-wrote the original screenplay with Sy Bartlett) to suit the style of Hope and Crosby. Hope would often look over scripts and decide if there were enough jokes. His wisecracking style had become quite popular on radio, and he was now a formidable name in films.

It would appear the Paramount brass chose *Find Colonel Fawcett* as the next Road picture due to its jungle setting. It was likely an attempt to capitalize on the immense popularity the Tarzan pictures were enjoying.

Victor Schertzinger, who directed this and the previous Road picture, had a career that dated back to silent pictures. He was actually a composer, having penned the score for Thomas Ince's *Civilization* (1916) as well as many other films. He began directing in 1917. This was his last directorial assignment with Bob Hope. A few months after *Road to Zanzibar* was released, Schertzinger died.

The critics generally liked *Road to Zanzibar*. Howard Barnes in *The New York Herald-Tribune* stated: "The *Road to Zanzibar* is nonsense, but it is nonsense of the most delightful sort."

Caught in the Draft

Directed by David Butler. Written by Wilkie C. Mahoney. Produced by B. G. DeSylva. Original Music by Frank Loesser and Victor Young. Lyricist: Louis Alter. Cinematography by Karl Struss. Film Editing by Irene Morra. Art Direction by Haldane Douglas and Hans Dreier. Costume Design by Edith Head. Makeup by Harry Ray. Sound Department: Gene Merritt and Walter Oberst.

Cast: Bob Hope (Don Bolton); Dorothy Lamour (Tony Fairbanks); Lynne Overman (Steve Riggs); Eddie Bracken (Bert Sparks); Clarence Kolb (Col. Peter Fairbanks); Paul Hurst (Sgt. Burns); Ferike Boros (Yetta); Phyllis Ruth (Margie); Irving Bacon (Cogswell); Phyllis Kennedy (Susan); Frank Marlowe (Twitchel); George McKay (Quartermaster Sergeant); Edgar Dearing (Recruiting Sergeant); Ray Flynn (Lieutenant Colonel); Weldon Heyburn (Sergeant at Examining Depot); Frank O'Connor (Major); Len Hendry (Corporal); Dave Willock (Colonel's Orderly); Frank Mitchell (Captain); Jack Luden (Captain); Jerry Jerome (Captain); Victor Cutler (Rookie); Jack Chapin (Rookie); George Lynn (Pilot); Andrew Tombes (Justice of the Peace); June Gittelson (Fat Girl); Arthur Loft (Director); Murray Alper (Make-up Man); David Oliver (Cameraman); Edward Hearn (Operation Manager); Heinie Conklin (Sign Hanger); Arch MacNair (Toothless Man); Edwin Stanley (Medical Examiner); Archie Twitchell (Stretcher Patient); Jimmie Dodd (Indignant Patient); Edward Peil, Jr. (Patient); Terry Ray (Patient); Frances Morris (Stretcher Nurse); Rita Owen (Cleaning Nurse); Ella Neal (Nurse); Earlene Heath (Nurse); Marie Blake (Nurse); Eleanor Stewart (Nurse); Gloria Williams (Nurse).

Released July 4, 1941, by Paramount Pictures.

Military comedies are a staple in cinema. While many are rife with clichés, it would seem that, as America prepared to enter the war in Europe, the Bob Hope character would be perfect as a military foil.

The Hope character is a wiseacre, balks at authority, avoids hard labor, chases women, and is generally a coward. All of these traits would serve an army comedy quite well and are the key points of the Hope screen persona.

Hence, putting Hope in an army setting, especially as war in Europe raged on, would appear to have strong international box office success.

Hope plays Don Bolton, a pampered movie star who wants to avoid being drafted. While America is not at war, the rigors of army life and basic training are enough to arouse his distaste. He proposes to Tony Fairbanks (Dorothy Lamour) only to discover that he is above the current age range for the draft and didn't have to bother. However, he and two cronies (Lynne Overman and Eddie Bracken) end up accidentally enlisting, after which they find themselves amid army procedure and under the command of Tony's father, the Colonel (Clarence Kolb).

Hope as a pampered star in *Caught in the Draft* (1941).

While it can be considered standard fare, *Caught in the Draft* makes the most of the typical army setting and gags. Most interesting are the bits of physical comedy that are not exactly the forte of fast-talking Hope. At one point, Hope finds himself in a women's dressing room. As the women undress, one complains of being a little overweight. Hope peeks through the curtain quickly, then shrugs. There is also a wild slapstick tank ride that includes Hope, Bracken, Overman, and a couple of women they pick up along the way.

The key to the film's success is Hope's classic portrayal of the back-pedaling coward whose smart quips and bravado are an obvious charade.

At the time Hope was making *Caught in the Draft*, the Nazis were storming the gates at Stalingrad and Japan was dominating the Pacific Rim. American involvement appeared inevitable. Hope had just finished his most successful radio season in the spring of 1941 and was given an honorary Oscar for "achievement in humanities and for his unselfish services to the motion picture industry." He also played service camps along the California coast, realizing the tremendous response army audiences offer. Hope arranged to have *Caught in the Draft* previewed at Camp Callan. It was a huge hit with the soldiers at its June preview and was equally embraced by civilian audiences upon its wide release July 4, 1941.

Hope is further benefited by a strong supporting cast. Dorothy Lamour had by this time become accustomed to Hope's ad-libbing and various methods of working, so she fit in nicely as the ingenue.

Clarence Kolb, a vaudeville veteran who had been part of the Kolb and Dill comedy team, had begun establishing himself as a character actor who specialized in appearing as blustery types. His performance as Colonel Fairbanks is tailor made for his talents. His long career spanned vaudeville, burlesque, movies, and television, with his recurring role as Mr. Honeywell on TV's *My Little Margie*. He died in 1964 at the age of 90.

Eddie Bracken is perhaps best known by modern audiences as Wally of Wally's World in *National Lampoon's Vacation*. His best work, however, appears in the Preston Sturges films *Hail the Conquering Hero* and *Miracle of Morgan's Creek*. He remained active in films and on stage until his death in 2002.

Caught in the Draft was Paramount's highest grossing film of 1941. *Time Magazine* stated:

> Bob Hope has made twelve pictures to date (three of them this year), has five more up and waiting. He is on NBC air every week for Pepsodent. If people grow weary of Hope's stylized impudence, it will largely be due to the star's appealing avarice.

Nothing but the Truth

Directed by Elliott Nugent. Writing Credits: Ken Englund and Don Hartman. From a story by James Montgomery. Based on the novel by Frederic S. Isham. Produced by Arthur Hornblow, Jr. Cinematography by Charles Lang. Film Editing by Alma Macrorie. Art Direction by Hans Dreier and Robert Usher. Costume Design by Edith Head. Sound Department: Richard Olson and Phil Wilson. Musical Director: Andrea Setaro. Process Photographer: Farciot Edouart.

Cast: Bob Hope (Steve Bennett); Paulette Goddard (Gwen Saunders); Edward Arnold (T. R. Ralston); Leif Erickson (Van); Helen Vinson (Linda Grahm); Willie Best (Samuel); Glenn Anders (Dick Donnelly); Grant Mitchell (Mr. Bishop); Catherine Doucet (Mrs. Van Dusen); Rose Hobart (Mrs. Donnelly); Clarence Kolb (Mr. Van Dusen); Mary Forbes (Mrs. Ralston); Leon Belasco (Dr. Zarak); Helene Millard (Miss Turner); Wilson Benge (Fredericks); Will Wright (Mr. Prichard); Rod Cameron (Sailor); Jack Chapin (Sailor); Lee Shumway (Cop); Jim Farley (Watchman); James Blaine (Doorman); Edward McWade (Elderly Clerk); Buck Woods (Porter); Eleanor Counts (Maid); Charlotte Craig (Receptionist); Jack Egan (Elevator Starter); Billy Dawson (Newsboy); Oscar Smith (Shoeshine Boy); Dick Chandler (Office Boy); Keith Richards (Boy); Victor Potel (Pedestrian).

Released October 10, 1941, by Paramount Pictures.

Hope plays Steve Bennett, a new partner in a stockbroking firm. His senior partner, T. R. Ralston (Edward Arnold) has recently made an agreement with his niece Gwen (Paulette Goddard). Ralston agrees that if Gwen can raise $20,000 for charity, he will match it. She has thus far raised $10,000 but is blocked from raising any more due to Ralston's influence on everyone she asks.

Gwen gives the money to Steve, asking that he attempt to double the amount. Steve foolishly bets the entire $10,000 that he can tell the truth for twenty-four hours. Having already accepted an invitation for a weekend on

T. R.'s houseboat, Steve is subjected to twenty-four hours of attempts to get him to lie or divulge the bet.

In their third film together, after the hugely successful *The Cat and the Canary* and *The Ghost Breakers*, that helped solidify Hope's movie star status; both Hope and Goddard breeze effortlessly through this pleasant, diverting comedy. Most of the laughs are derived from attempts to get Hope to lie and, therefore, lose the $10,000. Gags such as a dame masquerade by Hope and a few funny exchanges between him and Willie Best are among the highlights.

Best, who had also appeared with Hope and Goddard in *The Ghost Breakers*, has often been admonished for appearing as stereotypical characters, emphasizing the limits for African-American actors in Hollywood films of this era. However, people often overlook the real talent of Best and his contemporaries (Clarence Muse, Mantan Moreland, Stepin Fetchit, et al) refusing to look past what many label as being of racist intent in its presentation and execution. Of course, Best and his peers had established these characterizations over years on the black vaudeville circuit. In an interview, Mantan Moreland stated, "I was a comedian. If I wasn't afraid of ghosts, I wouldn't have been funny." Best remained active in films and television until his death in 1962.

Paulette Goddard was, at this time, being groomed for stardom outside of her work with Bob Hope. The one-time wife of Charlie Chaplin, who may be best known for appearing opposite him in *Modern Times* and *The Great Dictator*, Goddard also appeared in several of Cecil B. DeMille's films, once stating that she got those parts by flashing her feet at the fetishistic director!

Edward Arnold achieved perhaps his greatest success in the title role of *Diamond Jim* (1936) about the indulgent Diamond Jim Brady and his relationship with Lillian Russell. He was adept at appearing as stuffy business types in both dramas (*Mr. Smith Goes to Washington* [1939], *Johnny Eager* [1941]) and comedies such as this one. He is also quite enjoyable as the blustery mayor in the Martin and Lewis vehicle *Living It Up* (1954).

Nothing But the Truth is the sort of screwball comedy that was popular during the Depression and immediate pre-war period. It was a box office success, and succeeded in amusing even the hardest critics. Bosley Crowther in *The New York Times* stated:

> Honesty may be a policy of which the screen cannot always boast, but Paramount has certainly turned it to advantage — and to the further elevation of Bob Hope — in *Nothing But the Truth*. For here is an ancient farce comedy, already seen twice in films, which derives from an idea so obvious that it no longer supports a parlor game. Yet Paramount, plus director Elliot Nugent, plus the ever entangled Mr. Hope, kick it around so blithely and with such candid application of hokum, that you can't help find it amusing.

Louisiana Purchase

Directed by Irving Cummings. Written by Jerome Chodorov and Joseph Fields. From a short story by Buddy G. DeSylva. Based on the play by Morrie Ryskind. Produced by Harold Wilson. Original Music by Irving Berlin. Cinematography by Harry Hallenberger and Ray Rennahan. Film Editing by LeRoy Stone. Production Design by Raoul Pene Du Bois. Art Direction by Hans Dreier and Robert Usher. Costume Design by Raoul Pene Du Bois. Makeup by Wally Westmore. Sound by Earl S. Hayman and Walter Oberst. Musical Direction by Robert Emmett Dolan and Arthur Franklin. Color Consultants: Natalie Kalmus and Morgan Padelford.

Cast: Bob Hope (Jim Taylor); Vera Zorina (Marina Von Minden); Victor Moore (Senator Oliver P. Loganberry); Irene Bordoni (Madame Bordelaise); Dona Drake (Beatrice); Raymond Walburn (Colonel Davis, Sr.); Maxie Rosenbloom (The Shadow); Phyllis Ruth (Emmy Lou); Frank Albertson (Davis, Jr.); Donald MacBride (Captain Whitfield); Andrew Tombes (Dean Manning); Robert Warwick (Speaker of the House); Charles La Torre (Gaston); Charles Laskey (Danseur); Emory Parnell (Lawyer); Iris Meredith (Lawyer's Secretary); Joy Barlow (Girl Jester); Edgar Dearing (House Detective); John Hiestand (Radio Announcer); Shep Houghton (Singer/Dancer); Catherine Craig (Saleslady); Frances Gifford (Salesgirl); Sam McDaniel (Sam); Jack Norton (Jester); Donald Kerr (Jester); Patsy Mace (Girl Jester); Tom Patricola (Cab Driver); Floyd Shackelford (Nightclub Doorman); Dave Willock (Bellhop); Douglas Dean (Fuchsia Man); William Wright (Ambulance Driver); Jean Wallace, Louise La Planche, Barbara Slater, Eleanor Stewart, Alaine Brandes, Barbara Britton, Kay Aldridge, Blanche Grady, Lynda Grey, Margaret Hayes, Brooke Evans and Katharine Booth (Louisiana Belles).

Released December 25, 1941, by Paramount Pictures.

In his first Technicolor picture, Bob Hope tones down his characteristic wisecracking for a sober political satire based on the Broadway musical. Hope portrays Jim Taylor, an employee of the Louisiana Purchasing

Company who tries hard to avoid being blamed for the crooked acts of his superiors.

Victor Moore, Vera Zorina and Irene Bordoni all reprise their stage roles and add authenticity to Morrie Ryskind's deft satire (peppered with Irving Berlin tunes). While Hope was always particular about having enough jokes in the script, he plays it straight when necessary, with an obvious respect for the original material. His filibuster sequence, recalling James Stewart's similar scene in Frank Capra's *Mr. Smith Goes to Washington* (1939), is representative of his best work.

While it is hardly a typical Bob Hope comedy, *Louisiana Purchase* remains among his most interesting films. Its Broadway lineage and handsome Technicolor production, along with Hope's willingness to play a more subdued role than his established persona, offer an interesting, albeit atypical, presentation from this period of the comedian's film career.

Only two years earlier, Hope was still struggling through Paramount's B-picture unit. At the end of 1941, Hope was listed among the top five box office draws in the nation, after Mickey Rooney, Clark Gable, and Abbott and Costello. He would remain among the top ten at the box office for the next thirteen years and make it to number one in 1949.

My Favorite Blonde

Directed by Sidney Lanfield. Written by Frank Butler and Don Hartman. From a story by Melvin Frank and Norman Panama. Produced by Paul Jones. Original Music by David Buttolph. Cinematography by William C. Mellor. Film Editing by William Shea. Art Direction by Hans Dreier and Robert Usher. Costume Design by Edith Head. Makeup by Wally Westmore. Sound by Gene Garvin and Gene Merritt.

Cast: Bob Hope (Larry Haines); Madeleine Carroll (Karen Bentley); Gale Sondergaard (Madame Stephanie Runick); George Zucco (Dr. Hugo Streger); Lionel Royce (Karl); Walter Kingsford (Dr. Wallace Faber); Victor Varconi (Miller); Otto Reichow (Lanz); Esther Howard (Mrs. Topley); Edward Gargan (Mulrooney); James Burke (Union Secretary); Charles Cane (Turk O'Flaherty); Crane Whitley (Ulrich); Milton Parsons (Mortician); Erville Alderson (Sheriff); Tom Fadden (Tom Douglas); Leslie Denison (Elvan); Robert Emmett Keane (Nat Burton); Addison Richards (Herbert Wilson); Matthew Boulton (Col. Ashmont); Carl "Alfalfa" Switzer (Frederick); Isabel Randolph (Frederick's Mother); Paul Scardon (Dr. Robert Higby); Vernon Dent (Ole, Bartender); Jimmie Dodd (Stuttering Boy); Sarah Edwards (Mrs. Weatherwax); William Forrest (Col. Raeburn); Arno Frey (Male Nurse); Dick Elliott (Backstage Doorman); John Hiestand (Announcer); William Irving (Waiter); John Kelly and Lyle Latell (Bus Drivers); George Hickman (Elevator Boy); Teala Loring (Young Girl); Pearl Early (Hefty Woman); Rose Allen (Outraged Woman); Betty Farrington (Woman); Alice Keating (Woman); Nell Craig (Woman); Frank Mills (New York Cab Driver); Frank Marlowe (Chicago Cab Driver); Mike Lally (Chicago Taxi Driver); Leyland Hodgson (English Cab Driver); James Millican (Truck Driver); Kernan Cripps and Edmund Cobb (Yard Men); Wade Boteler (Conductor); Charles McAvoy (Brakeman); Charles R. Moore (Pullman Porter); Edward Hearn (Train Official); Dudley Dickerson (Red Cap); Dooley Wilson (Porter); Louis Natheaux (Man in Coffee Shop); Fred Kelsey (Sam, Policeman); Edgar Dearing (Joe, Policeman); Harry Hollingsworth (Irish Cop); Jack Clifford and Monte Blue (Policemen at Union Hall); Art Miles (Cop Outside Union Hall); Bing Crosby (Man Outside Union Hall; Bill Lally (Telegraph Operator); Kirby Grant,

Eddie Dew, George Turner and William Cabanne (Pilots); Max Wagner (Man with Truck); Lloyd Whitlock (Apartment Manager); Minerva Urecal (Stonefaced Woman); Jack Luden and Mary Akin (Spectators); Allan Ramsay, Johnny Erickson, Joe Recht, Gerald Pierce, David McKim and Rex Moore (Newsboys); Edward Peil, Sr. and Dick Rush (Cops).

Released March 18, 1942, by Paramount Pictures.

Once America had entered World War II, a new comic breed solidified itself in American movies. Talking pictures initially beckoned comedians from radio and the vaudeville stage, whose forte was smart quips and witty patter routines that hadn't translated well to silent pictures. The pantomime of the silent movie comedians was dying out. This was trouble for a comedian like Buster Keaton, whose career in talkies produced few films that ranked with his silent classics.

However, a comedian like Hope, who initially established stardom on radio and incorporated this success into a starring film career, was a perfect example of the new comic breed. The only other comedians who enjoyed the lofty box office status of Bob Hope during this period were Bud Abbott and Lou Costello. Abbott and Costello's wartime farces about military life as well as standard settings in haunted houses or the Wild West played up the rat-a-tat style of verbal comedy routines.

My Favorite Blonde was made after Hope had already firmly established himself as a movie and radio star. His solid footing among the top box office stars was proof of his enormous popularity, so the idea was to place Bob in a wartime setting. He had already done a comedy about army life, so the next best thing was to place him in jeopardy on the home front.

Writers Norman Panama and Melvin Frank wrote a screenplay on spec for Hope, basing it on Alfred Hitchcock's 1939 classic *The 39 Steps*. Hope liked the script so much that he used Panama and Frank frequently thereafter. He even went so far as to arrange that Madeleine Carroll, the star of *The 39 Steps*, be cast as his leading lady. Of course Hope also had his comedy writers Don Hartman and Frank Butler punch up the script with a plethora of jokes.

Carroll is cast as a beautiful spy who hooks up with small-time vaudevillian Hope (he works with a trained penguin) in order to use him to help deliver secret orders. The orders involve the shipment of war planes to her native England. A group of Nazis who want the plans for themselves are chasing her, so she uses Hope and his penguin as a decoy. Hope is initially unaware, being smitten by a pretty face. This leads to a cross-country chase and a series of amusing situations.

One of the film's highlights involves Hope's partner, Bing Crosby, in an unbilled cameo. Hope asks directions from Crosby, an idle bystander. After Hope walks away, he stops, thinks for a few seconds, then shrugs it off, "It couldn't be!"

Gale Sondergaard, fresh from her outstanding performance in Hitchcock's *Rebecca*, is great as a cold-hearted Nazi bent on wresting the papers from Hope and Carroll. George Zucco, a staple of horror films from this period, is equally welcome as Dr. Hugo Streger. Along with the familiar faces of Ed Gargan, James Burke, Fred Kelsey, and Vernon Dent, Carl "Alfalfa" Switzer makes an unbilled appearance in only his second film since outgrowing his long-time role in the "Our Gang" comedies.

My Favorite Blonde was a huge success, handily breaking all box office records at New York's Paramount Theater during a four-week run.

Road to Morocco

Directed by David Butler. Second Unit Director: Cullen Tate. Assistant Director: Hal Walker. Written by Frank Butler and Don Hartman. Produced by Paul Jones. Original Music by Jimmy Van Heusen and Johnny Burke. Cinematography by William C. Mellor. Film Editing by Irene Morra. Art Direction by Hans Dreier and Robert Usher. Costume Design by Edith Head. Makeup by Wally Westmore. Sound by Earl S. Hayman, Walter Oberst and Loren L. Ryder. Special Effects by Gordon Jennings.

Cast: Bing Crosby (Jeff Peters); Bob Hope (Orville "Turkey" Jackson/ Aunt Lucy); Dorothy Lamour (Princess Shalmar); Anthony Quinn (Mullay Kassim); Dona Drake (Mihirmah); Vladimir Sokoloff (Hyder Khan); Mikhail Rasumny (Ahmed Fey); George Givot (Neb Jolla); Yvonne De Carlo (Handmaiden); Monte Blue (Kassim's Aide); Andrew Tombes (Oso Bucco); Leon Belasco (Yusef, Undertaker); Cy Kendall (Fruit Vendor); Ken Maynard (Leader of Arab Horsemen); Suzanne Ridgeway (Handmaiden); Nestor Paiva (Sausage Vendor); Stanley Price (Idiot); Blue Washington (Nubian Slave); Poppy Wilde (Handmaiden); Sara Berner (Mabel, Voice of Lady Camel); Kent Rogers (Voice of Male Camel [voice]); Robert Barron (Giant Bearded Arab); Jamiel Hasson (Kassim's Aide); George Lloyd (Guard); Richard Loo (Chinese Announcer); Brandon Hurst (English Announcer); Pete G. Katchenaro (Filipino Announcer); Leo Mostovoy (Russian Announcer); Michael Mark (Pottery Vendor); Ralph Penney (Arabian Waiter); Dan Seymour (Slave Buyer); Nick Shaid (Arab Guard); Sammy Stein (Guard); Patsy Mace, Brooke Evans, Theo De Voe and Louise La Planche (Handmaidens); Edward Emerson (Bystander); Vic Groves and Joe Jewett (Knife Dancers); Rita Christiani (Specialty Dancer); Sylvia Opert (Dancer); Dick Botiller and Harry Cording (Warriors).

Released November 11, 1942, by Paramount Pictures.

Many consider *Road to Morocco* to be the best of the Road series. Some even go so far as to call it the best Bob Hope movie. While in good conscience this writer could not claim that it truly deserves either of these accolades, it is certainly one of the comedian's most enjoyable films.

Hope and Crosby are adrift on a raft, finally reach land, and hop a camel to an Arabian city. Crosby arranges to sell Hope into slavery but balks when he discovers that his buddy will be owned by beautiful Lamour and is slated to marry her. Bing, of course, tries to get in on the action, but as it turns out they have to contend with an evil Arab (Anthony Quinn) who has designs on Lamour himself.

As Bing and Bob ride a camel through the desert, they sing the title song. It contains the following lyrics:

> "Where we're going, why we're going, we cannot be sure,
> "I'll lay you 8 to 5 that we'll meet Dorothy Lamour!"

And:

> "Like Webster's Dictionary we're Morocco bound."

Along with the title song, two of the best tunes ever to be penned for a Road picture appear in *Road to Morocco*. These are "Moonlight Becomes You," which has become a standard, and "Ain't Got a Dime to My Name (Ho-Hum)," featuring Crosby at his best.

Like the previous two Road pictures, *Road to Morocco* is filled with jokes. As Hope and Crosby travel by camel through the desert, Hope quips, "This must be the place where they empty all the old hourglasses." In a dream sequence, Hope plays elderly Aunt Martha, who instructed Bing to watch over her nephew.

Not all of the comedy was scripted, and not all of the ad-libbing came from the stars. Early in the film, as Hope and Crosby prepare to ride the camel, the animal looked directly at Hope and spat into his face. His stunned reaction and Crosby's laughter were considered so amusing that the scene was left in the film.

Hope later stated that the smell of the camel's breath was so horrible he couldn't breathe. He does indeed stumble out of frame and Crosby ends the scene himself. Hope admitted that he was momentarily unable to catch his breath.

In another scene, Bing came to bed with his hat on, having failed to put on his toupee and not wanting to appear on film without it. Bob covered this by ad-libbing, "Do you always get your nightcaps from Stetson?"

Not all of the surprises were amusing. There was another sequence in which Hope and Crosby were chased down an alley by a herd of wild horses. The horses were let loose too early, and the actors were nearly trampled to death. They escaped, but the look of real terror in their eyes pleased director David Butler, so he used the footage in the finished film.

Hope, Dorothy Lamour and Bing Crosby (left to right) in *Road to Morocco* (1942).

Anthony Quinn, specializing in tough guys during this period of his career, had already appeared with Hope and Crosby in *Road to Singapore* and with Hope in *The Ghost Breakers*. While he would go on to offer tremendous performances in films like *La Strada, Viva Zapata, Requiem for a Heavyweight,* and *Zorba the Greek*, he never again appeared in a Bob Hope film.

Yvonne De Carlo appears, without billing, in a small part as a handmaiden in this, her fourth film appearance. Best known as Lily on television's *The Munsters*, she would appear in nearly one hundred feature films throughout her career.

When all was said and done, *Road to Morocco* emerged as the best Road picture thus far and was Hope's biggest hit to date. It was applauded by the critics as a fun entertainment to help take American moviegoers' minds off what was happening overseas. The public, hungering for light entertainment, embraced it with passion.

However, some retrospective reviews feel the film was not likely to hold up as well over time. The late Pauline Kael, film critic for *The New Yorker*, stated in her book *5001 Nights at the Movies*:

> Maybe you have to have seen the Bob Hope–Bing Crosby road movies (comedies with songs and a lot of patter) when they came out to understand the affection people felt for them and to appreciate how casually sophisticated the style seemed at the time. The pictures haven't weathered as well as 30s comedies because they were satirizing melodramas that are already forgotten. The series spoofed the fancy backgrounds of adventure movies; Hope and Crosby ambled through exotic, nonsensical lighthearted situations with no pretense to believability. They took the thud out of the dumb gags and topical jokes by their amiable comic intimacy. And the rare good jokes shone in the unpretentious atmosphere. Hope and Crosby's rapport has great charm, and every once in a while, Hope does something — a gesture or a dance movement — that is prodigiously funny. Dorothy Lamour is their joint inamorata and the foil of the series; inimitably out of it, she was taken over from the pictures being satirized, and she played in the same coy, easy-to-please manner.

Of course Kael's critical consensus that a film like *Road to Morocco* would date badly due to its topical references has been proven incorrect. In fact these references add a cultural value to the film's humor, and the movie's lack of pretension is the key to its continued success.

In 1996 *Road to Morocco* was selected by the National Film Preservation Board among those films to be preserved in the National Film Registry.

They Got Me Covered

Directed by David Butler. Assistant Director: John Sherwood. Written by Harry Kurnitz. From a story by Leonard Q. Ross and Leonard Spigelgass. Additional Dialog by Frank Fenton and Lynn Root. Produced by Samuel Goldwyn. Original Music by Harold Arlen, Leigh Harline and Johnny Mercer. Cinematography by Rudolph Maté. Film Editing by Daniel Mandell. Art Direction by Perry Ferguson. Set Decoration by Howard Bristol. Costume Design by Adrian and Edith Head. Production Management: Walter Mayo. Associate Art Director: McClure Capps. Sound by Fred Lau. Special Effects by Ray Binger. Marion Martin's singing voice is dubbed by Martha Mears.

Cast: Bob Hope (Robert Kittredge); Dorothy Lamour (Christina Hill); Lénore Aubert (Mrs. Vanescu); Otto Preminger (Fauscheim); Eduardo Ciannelli (Baldanacco); Marion Martin (Gloria); Donald Meek (Little Old Man); Phyllis Ruth (Sally); Philip Ahn (Nichimuro); Donald Mac-Bride (Mason); Mary Treen (Helen); Bettye Avery (Mildred); Margaret Hayes (Lucille); Mary Byrne (Laura); William Yetter, Sr. (Holtz [as William Yetter]); Henry Guttman (Faber); Florence Bates (Gypsy Woman); Walter Catlett (Hotel Manager); John Abbott (Vanescu); Don Brodie (Joe McGuirk); Hans Schumm (Schmidt); Frank Sully (Red); George Chandler (Smith); Etta McDaniel (Georgia); Greta Meyer (Katrina); Nino Pipitone (Testori); Henry Victor (Staeger); Kam Tong (Hawara); Wolfgang Zilzer (Cross); Arnold Stang (Drug Store Boy); Joe Devlin (Mussolini); Edward Gargan (Cop); Jack Carr (Comedian); Lillian Castle (Wardrobe Woman); Ferike Boros (Laughing Woman); Lane Chandler (Reporter); Stanley Clements (Office Boy); Hugh Prosser (Captain); Richard Keene (Reporter); Doris Day (Beautiful Girl in Sheet); Ralph Dunn (Cop); Willie Fung (Laundry Man); Peggy Lynn (Wardrobe Woman); Harry Bradley (Hotel Waiter); Eddie Hall (Navy Officer in Brawl; Donald Kerr (Stage Manager); Pat Lane (Ballet Dancer); Charles Legneur (Passenger in Plane); Lou Lubin (Bellboy); Tom Mazetti, Gil Perkins, Vic Mazetti and John Sinclair (Nazis); Bill O'Leary (Tramp); Anne O'Neal (Woman Patron); George Sherwood (Reporter); Byron Shores (FBI Man).

Released March 4, 1943, by Samuel Goldwyn Productions. Distributed
by RKO Pictures.

In Hope's first feature film away from Paramount, he was able to nego-
tiate a very sweet deal. Samuel Goldwyn wanted badly to make a picture with
Hope. So Hope instructed his agent, Al Melnick, to secure a $100,000 guar-
antee for the film plus a percentage of the profits. This made Hope one of
the highest paid movie actors in Hollywood.

Penned by Harry Kurnitz, who had written the popular Thin Man series
for MGM, *They Got Me Covered* is a generally amusing wartime comedy.

Bob plays Robert Kittredge, a reporter who has been fired after bungling
his latest assignment. He is further pressured by his lady friend Chris (Dorothy Lamour), who has been trying to push him into marriage. Kittredge
tries to save his job and his relationship when he gets a hot tip on some Nazi
spies operating in Washington, DC, and he convinces Chris to help him
break the story.

By the time he was shooting *They Got Me Covered*, Hope was already
noted for entertaining U.S. troops. As a wartime audience provided a ready
market for comedy, the film is filled with snappy period jokes. When watching this film today, one must be able to understand such lines as "Would
you bet a new tire?" that refer directly to the wartime rubber shortage.

Although it was his first film away from Paramount, *They Got Me Covered* is really no different from the sort of films he was making at his home
studio. The story was rather slight, the Goldwyn people apparently believing that Hope needed little more than a basis on which to hang funny lines.
Bosley Crowther of *The New York Times* noticed:

> As long as (Hope) has his gags, he's covered, no matter how slight
> the story is.

Variety also felt it was a notch below Hope's other films:

> A farce of the broadest stripe. Sometimes it takes and sometimes it
> doesn't. It's just too clear how hard the writers were trying. No asset to
> the film is the quality of much of the acting, particularly that of Dorothy
> Lamour. Director David Butler succeeds in keeping the film moving,
> despite the episodic construction of the situation gags.

While *Variety* appears to be unimpressed with the supporting players,
especially Ms. Lamour, the cast includes such familiar heavies as Otto Preminger; Eduardo Cianelli; and Lenore Aubert, who is best known as an
alluring vampire in *Abbott and Costello Meet Frankenstein* (Universal, 1948).
Ms. Lamour, who is often given little more than ingenue work in her Hope

films, fares just as well here as in any of the Paramount films in which she appears with the comedian.

David Butler directed at Hope's request, having already helmed *Caught in the Draft* and *Road to Morocco,* which were two of Bob's funnier comedies.

While shooting *They Got Me Covered,* Hope was asked by his friend and former stand-in Lyle Morain, an army sergeant, to take his camp show to Alaska. Eager to entertain the troops, Hope agreed to the assignment

They Got Me Covered wrapped on September 5. Never one to rest for very long, Hope left for Alaska on September 8. He performed a show for the servicemen at his friend's request but managed to squeeze this gig into his schedule quite comfortably.

By September 22, Hope had returned from the forty-eighth state and was ready to begin work on the new season of his radio show.

Let's Face It

Directed by Sidney Lanfield. Assistant Director: Lonnie D'Orsa. Writing Credits: Dorothy Fields, Herbert Fields, Harry Tugend, Cole Porter, Russell G. Medcraft and Norma Mitchell. Based on their play "Cradle Snatchers." Produced by Fred Kohlmar. Original Music by Cole Porter, Sammy Cahn and Jule Styne. Cinematography by Lionel Lindon. Film Editing by Paul Weatherwax. Art Direction by Hans Dreier and A. Earl Hedrick. Set Decoration by Ray Moyer. Sound by Hugo Grenzbach and Don Johnson.

Cast: Bob Hope (Jerry Walker); Betty Hutton (Winnie Porter); Zasu Pitts (Cornelia Figeson); Phyllis Povah (Nancy Collister); Dave Willock (Barney Hilliard); Eve Arden (Maggie Watson); Cully Richards (Frankie Burns); Marjorie Weaver (Jean Blanchard); Dona Drake (Muriel); Raymond Walburn (Julian Watson); Andrew Tombes (Judge Henry Pigeon); Arthur Loft (George Collister); Joe Sawyer (Sergeant Wiggins); Grace Hayle (Mrs. Wigglesworth); Evelyn Dockson (Mrs. Taylor); Lena Belle (Lena); Helena Brinton (Helena); Barbara Brooks (Barbara); Eddie Hall (Philip); Joyce Compton (Wiggins' Girl); Eddie Dew (Sergeant); Emory Parnell (Colonel); Frederic Nay (Walsh); Barbara Pepper (Daisy); Ellen Johnson (Ellen); Robin Raymond (Mimi); Debbra Keith (Betty); Phyllis Ruth (Lulu); William B. Davidson (Man in Boat); Eddie Dunn (Cop); Brooke Evans (Milkmaid); Elinor Troy (Elinor); Kay Linaker (Canteen Hostess); George Meader (Justice of the Peace); Andria Moreland (Milkmaid); Yvonne De Carlo (Chorus Girl); Noel Neill, Julie Gibson and Jayne Hazard (as Girls); Eleanore Prentiss (Woman in Court); Cyril Ring (Head Waiter); Lionel Royce (Submarine Commander); Florence Shirley (Woman in Sun Shell Cafe); Jerry James, Hal Rand and Allen Ray (bit parts); Donald Kerr (Specialty Dancer).

Released August 5, 1943, by Paramount Pictures.

Let's Face It was originally a Broadway musical, with Danny Kaye in the Hope role. It was retailored by Harry Tugend into a typical Hope vehicle. This is one of the least-seen Bob Hope movies, having been generally out of circulation for some time. Even some of the most passionate fans of Bob Hope have not seen *Let's Face It*. There is no official reason for its lack of availability.

It is yet another service-oriented comedy, Hope not forgetting his massive popularity among soldiers. He plays GI Jerry Walker, whose girl Winnie (Betty Hutton) works as a drill instructor for overweight women. Jerry will make extra money by quietly selling junk food to her portly charges. Winnie wants to get married, but Jerry keeps hocking the ring ("We may have to spend our honeymoon in the pawnshop"). Three women (Eve Arden, Zasu Pitts, Phyllis Povah), tired of their husbands' philandering, decide to turn the tables by hooking up with three young escorts. Jerry, in need of cash for his impending marriage as well as for a repair bill for an army jeep he ruined, recruits two GI pals in an effort to make extra money. (While Pitts and Povah were both around fifty at the time of filming, Arden was only thirty-five—five years younger than Hope!)

Perhaps part of the reason *Let's Face It* is so little seen today is due to its dated sexism. When Hope first approaches the exercise class of overweight women from behind the bushes he looks to the camera and quips, "How can they have so much and the butcher shops so little," referring directly to the wartime meat shortage. When he is caught selling treats to the women, Winnie chastises him by stating, "I'm trying to trim those blimps down!"

The three frumpy women seem to simply take for granted that their husbands are "cutie chasing." They also discuss wanting to keep their husbands, despite this philandering. "They're the only husbands we have, and we're going to hang onto them!" While they are presented as terribly unattractive to Jerry and his pals, their equally frumpy husbands easily hook up with young beautiful girls. At one point, one of Jerry's pals, ready to help him earn extra money, states, "Jerry to help you out of a jam I'd kiss a pig." Whereupon Jerry replies, "You may have to!" Upon first seeing the women, Jerry's pals state, "I've seen better heads on glasses of beer" and "I didn't know Boris Karloff had a grandmother!"

When Jerry and the boys hitch a ride on the back of a truck, they get out at their destinations and holler, "Thanks Mac!" When they discover it is a woman doing the driving, they are surprised: "And we were riding in the back!" "Gee, they do everything now, don't they?" This is in reference to the wartime man shortage that brought women into the workplace.

Of course this sort of humor was not an issue of political correctness during these times, so it wasn't looked upon as even mildly offensive.

The situations in *Let's Face It* are pretty standard, one of the chief highlights being a physical bit in which Jerry and his pals pose as statues in order to sneak past their sergeant (Joe Sawyer).

There are plenty of Hope's trademark quips. When Jerry leaves to hook up with the older women, he tells Winnie he is going on an important secret mission. "Men have been known to get shot doing what I'm about to do."

It is unfortunate that this was the only film in which Hope is cast opposite the always appealing Betty Hutton. In a much later TV interview with Robert Osborne on the Turner Classic Movies cable television network, Ms. Hutton recalled that Hope felt her presence was so strong on film, it could easily eclipse his. He did, however, use her often on his radio show.

While filming *Let's Face It*, Hope was asked to put his hand and footprints in the entrance area at Grauman's Chinese Theater. He also dipped his famous ski-slope nose in the wet cement and quipped "If it hardens I won't be able to blow it for months."

The Princess and the Pirate

Directed by David Butler and Sidney Lanfield. Story by Sy Bartlett. Adaptation by Allen Boretz and Curtis Kenyon. Screenplay by Everett Freeman, Don Hartman and Melville Shavelson. Produced by Samuel Goldwyn. Associate Producer: Don Hartman. Original Music by Harold Adamson, Jimmy McHugh and David Rose. Cinematography by Victor Milner and William Snyder. Film Editing by Daniel Mandell. Art Direction by McClure Capps and Ernst Fegté. Set Decoration by Howard Bristol. Assistant Director: Barton Adams. Sound by Fred Lau. Special Effects by R. O. Binger and Clarence Slifer.

Cast: Bob Hope (Sylvester the Great); Virginia Mayo (Princess Margaret); Walter Brennan (Featherhead); Walter Slezak (La Roche); Victor McLaglen (The Hook); Marc Lawrence (Pedro); Hugo Haas (Cafe Owner); Maude Eburne (Landlady); Adia Kuznetzoff (Don Jose); Brandon Hurst (Mr. Pelly); Tom Kennedy (Alonzo); Stanley Andrews (Captain of the Mary Ann); Robert Warwick (The King); Jack Carr (Bartender); Tom Tyler (Lieutenant); Alma Carroll (Handmaiden); Colin Kenny (First Mate on the Mary Ann); Ralph Dunn (Murderous Pirate); Francis Ford (Drunken Pirate); Bert Roach (Companion of Drunken Pirate); Edwin Stanley (Captain of the King's Ship); Sammy Stein (Black Jack Thug); James Flavin (Naval Officer); Al Bridge, Al Hill, Mike Mazurki, Dick Rich (Pirates); Oscar "Dutch" Hendrian (Heckler); Rondo Hatton (Gorilla); Weldon Heyburn and Edward Peil, Sr. (Palace Guards); Ray Teal (Guard); Frank Moran (Heckler); Richard Alexander (Holdup Man); Ruth Valmy (Handmaiden); Crane Whitley (Soldier); Ernie Adams, Robert Hale and Constantine Romanoff (Citizens); Ted Billings, Bill Hunter, Stewart Garner, Vic Christy, Art Miles (bit parts); Bing Crosby (Cameo Appearance); The Goldwyn Girls (Loretta Daye, Betty Alexander, Betty Thurston, Ruth Caldwell, Kay Morley, Lillian Molieri).

Released November 17, 1944, by Samuel Goldwyn Productions. Distributed by RKO Pictures.

Hope's next film for Goldwyn was a beautifully mounted Technicolor production. Dissatisfied with the average quality of his past couple of films, Hope made sure *The Princess and the Pirate* was filled with jokes from members of his writing staff like Melville Shavelson and Don Hartman. The idea worked, and *The Princess and the Pirate* remains one of his very best films.

Hope plays Sylvester the Great, *Man of Seven Faces*, a master of disguise traveling by ship. When the ship is captured and overrun with pirates led by the Hook (Victor McLaglen), he dons the disguise of an elderly woman and escapes with the help of pirate Featherhead (Walter Brennan) and a beautiful princess (Virginia Mayo), who is on the lam because

Hope as Sylvester the Great in *The Princess and the Pirate* (1944).

she loves a commoner. The pirates are aware of the princess's identity and want to hold her for a king's ransom. Featherhead has given Sylvester a treasure map that the Hook is also after. Rather than give it to Sylvester on paper, however, he tattoos it on Sylvester's chest as he sleeps.

The Princess and the Pirate is essentially a madcap chase, with Sylvester and the princess trying to make their way to safety so that the princess can be reunited with the commoner she loves. In one highlight, Sylvester tries to raise money by performing his act in a tough town, but it is the princess's beauty as his assistant who wins over the customers. In another, Sylvester and the princess are staying at the home of Governor La Roche (Walter Slezak), who is good friends with the Hook. When the Hook also comes to visit, he does not recognize Sylvester without the old lady makeup he'd been wearing when he escaped the ship.

Perhaps the most amusing sequence features Sylvester dressed up as the Hook while hiding on the pirate ship. Sylvester comes out and orders his crew to bring the princess to him. Then the actual Hook appears and orders that they put her in irons. This goes on back and forth until the Hook realizes something is amiss. McLaglen and Hope then engage in the old shaving pantomime, where Sylvester feels he is looking into a mirror when it is in fact the Hook looking through a porthole and matching his every move.

The Princess and the Pirate is filled with truly memorable sequences and remains among the very best Bob Hope movies. However, it is the film's ending that seems to especially stay with the viewer.

When the princess finally makes it home, the treasure is safe, and the Hook is captured, her father grants her permission to marry her commoner. It turns out to be Bing Crosby in a cameo. Hope quips, "I do all the work for ten reels and some extra from Paramount gets the girl. This is the last picture I do for Goldwyn!"

And it was.

Road to Utopia

Directed by Hal Walker. Writing Credits: Melvin Frank and Norman Panama. Produced by Paul Jones. Original Music by Leigh Harline, Jimmy Van Heusen and Johnny Burke. Non-Original Music by Heinz Roemheld. Cinematography by Lionel Lindon. Art Direction by Roland Anderson and Hans Dreier. Set Decoration by George Sawley. Costume Design by Edith Head. Makeup by Wally Westmore. Assistant Director: Alvin Ganzer. Sound by Hugo Grenzbach and Philip Wisdom. Special Effects by Farciot Edouart and Gordon Jennings. Dance Director: Danny Dare.

Cast: Bing Crosby (Duke Johnson); Bob Hope (Chester Hooton); Dorothy Lamour (Sal Van Hoyden); Hillary Brooke (Kate); Douglass Dumbrille (Ace Larson); Jack LaRue (LeBec); Robert Barrat (Sperry); Nestor Paiva (McGurk); Robert Benchley (On-Screen Narrator); Will Wright (Mr. Latimer); Larry Daniels and Jimmie Dundee (Ringleaders); Edward Emerson (Emcee); Al Ferguson (Cop); Art Foster (Husky Sailor); Charles Gemora (Bear); Arthur Loft (Purser); Jimmy Lono (Eskimo); Ferdinand Munier (Santa Claus); Romaine Callender (Top Hat); Stanley Andrews (Joe, Official at Boat); Al Bridge (Boat Captain); Paul Newlan (Tough Ship's Purser); Ronald R. Rondell (Hotel Manager); Lee Shumway (Cop); Jack Stoney and Allen Pomeroy (Henchmen); Jim Thorpe (Passenger); Bobby Barber, Pat West and Frank Moran (Bartenders); George McKay (Waiter); George Anderson (Townsman); William "Billy" Benedict (Newsboy); Charles C. Wilson and Edgar Dearing (Officials); Brandon Hurst, Don Gallaher and Bud Harrison (Men at Zambini's); Eddie Hall (Man in Saloon Behind Hope and Crosby); Jack Rutherford and Al Hill (Men); Claire James and Maxine Fife (Girls); Ethan Laidlaw (Saloon Extra).

Released March 22, 1946, by Paramount Pictures.

Road to Utopia is such a brisk, funny comedy that it matches the high standard set by *Road to Morocco*.

There was some delay in getting this film in production. By this time, Hope, Crosby, and Lamour were such big stars, the screenwriters had to work hard to appease each of them.

This is the first Road picture screenplay not written by Frank Butler and Don Hartman. The assignment was instead given to Hope's radio writers, Norman Panama and Mel Frank, who had penned the original story for *My Favorite Blonde*.

The screenwriters presented their screenplay for *Road to Utopia* to each of the stars separately. When they spoke to Bing, they made it sound like he was the star. When they told the story to Bob, they emphasized his point of view. Once each of them gave approval, Dorothy was sold.

Hope and Crosby play vaudevillians Duke and Chester who go to Alaska to join the gold rush. While stowing away on the ship they find a map to a secret gold mine that had been stolen by a couple of thugs (Robert Barrat and Nestor Paiva). They disguise themselves as the thugs to get off the ship. Meanwhile, a woman (Dorothy Lamour) is in Alaska searching for the map to the gold mine, as it originally belonged to her father.

Some of the Road series' funniest scenes occur in *Road to Utopia*. While on board ship, Duke loses a talent show. Chester then quips, "Next time I'll bring Sinatra!" This is at a time when Crosby's popularity was slowly being eclipsed by the rising young crooner (just as Elvis Presley would eclipse Sinatra ten years later).

However some latter-day critics, most notably the *New Yorker*'s Pauline Kael, believe such references are too topical and tend to date the film. In her book *5001 Nights at the Movies* she stated:

> Some of the patter is pure, relaxed craziness, but the topical jokes (about Paramount Pictures; about Crosby's rivalry with Frank Sinatra; about Hope's radio sponsor, a toothpaste company) keep pulling it down.

The pace is kept moving by the wry commentary of Robert Benchley, who appears on screen a couple of times as an onlooker narrating the story as it is presented in flashback. At one point, when observing a team of sled dogs, he comments, "The lead dog is the only one that ever gets a change of scenery."

In another highlight, Hope and Crosby sing one of their most memorable duets, "Put 'er there Pal" in which Hope sings, "I saw *Dixie*" and Crosby responds, "And I saw *Let's Face It*" each referring to a less-successful film by the other.

Hope always fondly recalled the sequence where he and Crosby enter a tough saloon. Chester orders a lemonade. When the bartender (Douglass Dumbrille) reacts, Chester demonstrates his toughness by demanding the soft drink be served "in a dirty glass!"

If this isn't enough, a touch of surrealism occurs via Lew Lehr's talking

Bing Crosby, Dorothy Lamour and Hope (left to right) in *Road to Utopia* (1946).

animal sequences, using an odd blend of animation and live action long before digital effects were available.

As with *Road to Morocco*, there was real danger performing some of the sequences in *Road to Utopia*. In one sequence, Bob and Bing had to climb a rope up the side of the glacier and the rope was to break. They were using a fairly high wall, and mattresses were put at the bottom to break their fall in case of an accident. The rope did indeed break, but someone had moved the mattresses. Bing fell, and Bob landed on top of him. Due to this mishap, Bing developed chronic back pain that would plague him for the rest of his life.

In another dangerous sequence Hope and Crosby are sleeping under a rug where a tame grizzly bear was to sniff around. Instead, however, the bear planted himself heavily atop the rug concealing the two actors and began snarling and clawing at it. The trainer stepped in and chained the animal up, insisting that they were in no danger. One day later, the bear lost control and tore the arm off the trainer!

Critics celebrated the release of *Road to Utopia* as did moviegoers. Bosley Crowther in *The New York Times* stated:

> Not since Chaplin was prospecting for gold in a Hollywood made many long years ago has so much howling humor been swirled with so much artificial snow. It will skyrocket laughter throughout the land.

Moviegoers made the film one of the top box office attractions of 1945.

Road to Utopia also has perhaps the most memorable ending of any Bob Hope picture. The finale takes place years later with an elderly Chester and Sal (Lamour) married and at home. There is a knock on the door, and an elderly Duke enters (he was presumed dead). He reacquaints himself with his old friends. Sal then asks, "Would you like to see our son?" Chester calls for "Junior," who enters. It is a young Bing Crosby. An embarrassed Duke looks away. Chester looks at the screen and explains, "We adopted him!"

In an interview with Gary Schneeberger decades later, Hope still marveled at how they got this suggestive sequence past the censors of the period. "I guess the line 'we adopted him' is what saved us."

Hope was not above being risqué, and often his double entendres on his radio show would be so blue, he would abruptly be censored and replaced by organ music. During the period when shock comic Andrew Dice Clay was popular, Hope admitted to finding him funny and that he was a long-time fan of "locker room stories."

However, the censorship limitations in films after 1934 and before the post-war era were very restrictive. Hope may have playfully attempted to sneak a few things past the censors, but this final sequence is perhaps the only time he was successful, at least until a later film like *Boy, Did I Get a Wrong Number!* which was made in 1966 and allowed for somewhat more freedom.

Road to Utopia is the one film in the series in which Hope gets Lamour. Unfortunately, the ending seems to indicate that Bing got her first.

Perhaps if one were to be initially introduced to the films of Bob Hope, *Road to Utopia* would be the most effective checkpoint. It features everything good about the humor of Bob Hope and the real joy of the Road pictures.

Opposite page: Ad for *Road to Utopia*, 1946.

Monsieur Beaucaire

Directed by George Marshall. Written by Melvin Frank, Norman Panama and Frank Tashlin. From a novel by Booth Tarkington. Produced by Paul Jones. Original Music by Robert Emmett Dolan, Ray Evans and Jay Livingston. Cinematography by Lionel Lindon. Film Editing by Arthur P. Schmidt. Art Direction by Hans Dreier and A. Earl Hedrick. Set Decoration by Sam Comer and Ross Dowd. Costume Design by Mary Kay Dodson and Gile Steele. Makeup Department: Wally Westmore. Assistant Director: Edward Salven. Sound by Don Johnson and Gene Merritt. Special Effects by Farciot Edouart and Gordon Jennings.

Cast: Bob Hope (Monsieur Beaucaire); Joan Caulfield (Mimi); Patric Knowles (Duc le Chandre); Marjorie Reynolds (Princess Maria of Spain); Cecil Kellaway (Count D'Armand); Joseph Schildkraut (Don Francisco); Reginald Owen (King Louis XV); Constance Collier (The Queen of France); Hillary Brooke (Mme. Pompadour); Fortunio Bonanova (Don Carlos); Douglass Dumbrille (George Washington); Mary Nash (The Duenna); Leonid Kinskey (Rene); Howard Freeman (King Philip); Charles Coleman (Major Domo); Eric Alden (Swordsman); Helen Freeman (Queen of Spain); John Berkes (Court Jester); Alan Hale, Jr. (Courtier); Anthony Caruso (Masked Horseman); Lane Chandler (Officer); John Mylong (Minister of State); Noreen Nash (Baroness); Audrey Wilder (Countess); Catherine Craig (Duchess); Brandon Hurst (Marquis); Mona Maris (Marquisa Velasquez); Nina Borget (Wife); Robert "Buddy" Shaw (Husband); Yola d'Avril (Housekeeper); Jean De Briac (Minister of Finance); Jean Del Val (Minister of War); Antonio Filauri (Minister of Navy); Lewis L. Russell (Chief Justice); William Frambes (Page); Carl Neubert (Baron); Martin Garralaga (Servant); Eddie Hall (Second Masked Horseman); Len Hendry (Spanish Officer); Nan Holliday (Maid in Waiting); Sol Gorss (Swordsman Bandit); Bert LeBaron and George Bruggeman (Bandits); George Lynn (Soldier); Lynne Lyons (Signora Gonzales); Sherry Hall (Sentry); John Maxwell (Courtier); George Sorel (Duke); Nanette Vallon (Maid in Waiting); Tony Paton (Waiter); Nino Pipitone (Lackey); Hugh Prosser (Courtier); Torben Meyer (Count); Victor Romito, George Magrill, Rudy Germaine, Jack Mulhall, Charles Cooley, William Meader,

Philip Van Zandt, and Crane Whitley (Guards); Buddy Roosevelt and Manuel París (Spanish Guards); Dorothy Vernon (Servant); Ralph Navarro (Thin Man).

Released September 4, 1946, by Paramount Pictures.

Comedian Woody Allen has often cited Bob Hope as a major inspiration, using *Monsieur Beaucaire* as an example of Hope at his best. In fact, Allen's *Love and Death* (1975) is generally an homage to this swashbuckling spoof.

Loosely based on the similarly titled Rudolph Valentino silent, Hope plays the title role, a royal barber during the sixteenth century. Beaucaire gets into royal trouble and thus is sent on a veritable suicide mission where he must impersonate a nobleman, the Duc Le Chandre, or lose his head. Meanwhile, in Madrid, Don Francisco, commander-in-chief of the Spanish army, wants to thwart the upcoming marriage of the actual Le Chandre (Patric Knowles) to Maria (Margaret Lindsay), a Spanish princess. Beaucaire is successful enough with his impersonation of Le Chandre, thus becoming the victim of Francisco and his men, who plan to assassinate the nobleman.

Monsieur Beaucaire is the perfect vehicle for Hope. His character works best when he is back-pedaling through dangerous territory, and *Monsieur Beaucaire* places the title character in a series of life-threatening situations.

It is interesting to compare this film to the original Rudolph Valentino vehicle, which was much closer to the Booth Tarkington novel. In the silent, Beaucaire is, himself, a courageous man; impersonating Le Chandre of his own choosing and bravely standing up for the nobleman and fighting his battles. Norman Panama and Mel Frank do a very nice job of altering the story so that the title character is instead forced into the ruse and will emerge as a comical coward in dangerous situations.

Producer Paul Jones, who'd often worked with Hope, was not particularly impressed with the screenplay by Panama and Frank. He felt the script was bland and did not feature enough humor inherent in the situations. Even after Hope's gaggle of joke writers went through the script and added the comedian's asides, Jones felt the screenplay was not strong enough.

Jones hired comedy writer Frank Tashlin to punch up Panama and Frank's script. Tashlin had cut his teeth on animated cartoons at the Warner Brothers studios, putting the likes of Bugs Bunny and Daffy Duck through their paces. Once he came into live-action films, he often used outrageous, even surreal, gags in his comedies, stemming from his having worked in animation. Tashlin felt that the freedom of animated gags could be translated to live action with some nod to the special effects department (it should be remembered that special effects were far more primitive, without the computer technology used regularly today).

Tashlin's first live-action screen work involved adding to already established scripts, such as his contribution to *Monsieur Beaucaire*. Eventually he began doing second-unit direction on some comedy sequences (including the wild chase in Hope's 1950 feature *My Favorite Spy*) as well as directing some outrageously funny comedies [including one of Hope's best, *Son of Paleface* (1952)].

Tashlin is best known for directing some of Jerry Lewis's best films (including *Artists and Models*, *The Geisha Boy*, *It's Only Money*, *Who's Minding the Store*), greatly influencing Lewis's own surreal directorial style. Tashlin also helmed some interesting attacks on Hollywood and show business, including *Will Success Spoil Rock Hunter* and *The Girl Can't Help It*.

Despite Tashlin's talent with comedy, Panama and Frank felt they had been cast aside and complained to the Writer's Guild. The Guild supported them, as did Hope, who felt the script was fine and that it just needed the jokes, which were easily provided by his staff. This caused a delay in production. Hope was very eager to get started, so he convinced studio head Henry Ginsberg to go ahead with the Panama-Frank script as written. Ginsberg was a no-nonsense sort, often interested in efficiency and budget cutting. He could hardly have been pleased by a delay in production.

The filming was completed, and the first preview audience proved that producer Paul Jones had been correct. There were hardly any laughs, and the pacing seemed slow. As a result, Tashlin was hired to write and direct some additional scenes that could easily be edited into the finished film.

It is Tashlin's contribution that resulted in the success for *Monsieur Beaucaire*. Bosley Crowther wrote in *The New York Times*:

> It's a cinch the late Booth Tarkington would not have remotely recognized his *Monsieur Beaucaire* in the picture of that title which came to the Paramount (theater) yesterday. His yarn was a ruff and rapier romance, and the films is, well, call it straight burlesque. But considering that Mr. Tarkington was a fellow who liked a hearty jest, he would probably have howled at the picture, just the same as everyone else will.

Variety, however, felt the film went too far over the top:

> Booth Tarkington's costume novel about a court barber forced to impersonate royalty has plenty of giggles and a few solidly promised laughs. Bob Hope plays the French barber Beaucaire with all stops out, waltzes through trying situations and varied romances with a bravado that is his particular forte. It's all fun, but could have been more so if treated with a bit less broadness.

Audiences disagreed, and *Monsieur Beaucaire* was another huge box office success. The war had ended, and post-war audiences wanted pure escapism even more now than when the troops were fighting overseas. Bob Hope's status at the box office remained firm.

My Favorite Brunette

Directed by Elliott Nugent. Story and screenplay by Edmund Beloin and Jack Rose. Produced by Daniel Dare. Original Music by Robert Emmett Dolan, Ray Evans and Jay Livingston. Cinematography by Lionel Lindon. Film Editing by Ellsworth Hoagland. Art Direction by Hans Dreier and A. Earl Hedrick. Set Decoration by Sam Comer and John MacNeil. Costume Design by Edith Head. Makeup by Wally Westmore. Assistant Director: Mel Epstein. Sound by Gene Garvin and Harold Lewis. Special Effects by Gordon Jennings and Farciot Edouart.

Cast: Bob Hope (Ronnie Jackson); Dorothy Lamour (Carlotta Montay); Peter Lorre (Kismet); Lon Chaney, Jr. (Willie); John Hoyt (Dr. Lundau); Charles Dingle (Maj. Simon Montague); Reginald Denny (James Collins); Frank Puglia (Baron Montay); Ann Doran (Miss Rogers); Willard Robertson (Prison Warden); Jack La Rue (Tony); Charles Arnt (Oliver J. Crawford); Jean Wong (Mrs. Fong); Roland Soo Hoo (Baby Fong); Alan Ladd (Sam McCloud); Garry Owen and Richard Keene (Reporters); Boyd Davis (Mr. Dawson); James Flavin (Detective Lt. Mac Hennessey); Brandon Hurst (Butler); Ted Rand (Waiter Captain); Charles Cooley (Waiter); Jack Chefe (Henri, Headwaiter); Tom Dillon (Cop); Helena Phillips Evans (Mabel, Cleaning Lady); Betty Farrington (Matron); Budd Fine (Detective); Ray Teal and Al Hill (State Troopers); John Westley (Doctor); James Pierce (Detective); George Lloyd (George, Prison Guard Sergeant); Eddie Johnson (Caddy); Reginald Simpson (Assistant Hotel Manager); John Tyrrell (Bell Captain); Harland Tucker (Room Clerk); Joe Recht (Newsboy); Anthony Caruso (First Man on Death Row); Clarence Muse (Second Man on Death Row); Matt McHugh (Third Man on Death Row).

Released March 14, 1947, by Paramount Pictures.

My Favorite Brunette is another of Hope's best films, maintaining his solid cinematic winning streak.

Hope plays baby photographer Ronnie Jackson, on death row and ready to be executed. He agrees to tell his story to reporters, and, as he narrates, flashbacks recall what happened.

Ronnie was reasonably successful as a baby photographer but longed for the excitement and romance of detective work. While hanging around in the office of a neighboring private eye, Ronnie is mistaken for the sleuth by the beautiful Carlotta Montay (Dorothy Lamour) and asked to help her find her missing uncle, the Baron. Wanting to be a detective, Ronnie agrees and finds himself mixed up in a plot to steal the map to a valuable uranium mine.

My Favorite Brunette is filled with highlights, but one of its strongest factors is its supporting cast.

Peter Lorre is at his sinister best. Lorre always had a knack for being able to place his noted screen persona in either comic or dramatic settings and still have the desired effect. In something as outrageous as *The Boogie Man Will Get You,* Lorre is able to use his character for laughs, while a comedy like *Arsenic and Old Lace* (1944) has him appearing essentially straight within the confines of an outrageous comedy. With the Hope film, Lorre is the villain off whom the cowardly Hope character can play. The connection is superb.

Lon Chaney, Jr., was already a star of horror films, based on his career-defining performance in the Universal Studios horror classic *The Wolf Man* (1941). In *My Favorite Brunette,* Chaney decides to channel his Oscar-nominated role as the slow-witted Lenny in *Of Mice and Men* (1939) and play it for laughs.

As with most of Hope's best comedies, *My Favorite Brunette* is filled with funny quips. During the opening baby photographer scenes, Ronnie is struggling to get a child to smile, but to no avail. He comments, "This kid's gonna grow up to be a sponsor!"

When Ronnie goes to call on the neighboring private eye, he begs for a position, stating he wants to be a detective like the ones in the movies and citing Alan Ladd as an example. The private eye turns around, and it is Alan Ladd in a surprise cameo.

When Ronnie is trapped in an asylum, he tries to outsmart Willie (Lon Chaney, Jr.) into bending the window bars so that he can escape. Willie does so, but then bends them back into place, stating, "Ya gotta be neat, y'know." When Ronnie tries to display his own strength, Willie feels the photographer's muscle and exclaims, "It's just like a woman, ain't it." Hope even calls attention to Chaney's similar performance in *Of Mice and Men* when, after asking Willie to bend the window bars, he states, "I'll buy you a rabbit."

Perhaps the funniest scene comes at the end. The flashback has ended, and the reporters, upon hearing the story, realize that Ronnie is innocent, as do the powers that be. Hence, he is released from death row. Enter Bing

Crosby in an unbilled cameo as the executioner, exhibiting anger at not being able to fry Hope. Hope looks directly into the camera and states, "He'll take any kind of a part!"

Crosby did this cameo for $25,000, all of which he donated to charity.

Where There's Life

Directed by Sidney Lanfield. Writing by Allen Boretz and Melville Shavelson. Produced by Paul Jones. Original Music by Charles Bradshaw and Van Cleave. Non-Original (Stock) Music by Daniele Amfitheatrof, David Buttolph, Gerard Carbonara, Robert Emmett Dolan, John Leipold, Joseph J. Lilley and Victor Young. Cinematography by Charles B. Lang, Jr. Film Editing by Archie Marshek. Art Direction by Hans Dreier and Earl Hedrick. Set Decoration by Sam Comer and Sydney Moore. Costume Design by Edith Head. Makeup by Wally Westmore. Assistant Directors: Oscar Rudolph and Edward Salven. Sound by John Cope and Hugo Grenzbach. Special Effects by Farciot Edouart and Gordon Jennings.

Cast: Bob Hope (Michael Joseph Valentine); Signe Hasso (Gen. Katrina Grimovitch); William Bendix (Victor O'Brien); George Coulouris (Prime Minister Krivoc); Vera Marshe (Hazel O'Brien); George Zucco (Paul Stertorius); Dennis Hoey (Minister of War Grubitch); John Alexander (Mr. Herbert Jones); Victor Varconi (Finance Minister Zavitch); Joseph Vitale (Albert Miller); Harry von Zell (Joe Snyder); Anthony Caruso (John Fulda); Norma Varden (Mabel Jones); Harland Tucker (Mr. Alvin); Emil Rameau (Dr. Josefsberg); William Edmunds (King Hubertus II); John Mallon (Mordian); Leo Mostovoy (Minister of Interior Karakovic); Oscar O'Shea (Uncle Philip); Hans von Morhart (Karl); Ernö Verebes (Peter Gornics); Floyd Pruitt, Pat Flaherty, Bud Sullivan and Jack Clifford, William Haade, Tom Coleman and John Jennings (An O'Brien); Fred Zendar (Co-pilot); Eric Alden (Airport Attendant); Edgar Dearing (Desk Sergeant); Edwin Chandler (New York Police Officer); Rene Dussaq and Charles Legneur (Officers); Jimmie Dundee, George Lloyd and Ralph Peters (Cops); Mary Field (Hotel Maid); Roy Atwell (Salesman); Brandon Hurst (Floor Walker); Lorna Jordon (Salesgirl); Phyllis Kennedy (Hotel Maid); Guy Kingsford (Mordian Pilot); Dario Piazza, Ralph Gomez, Otto Reichow, Gene Roth and Charles Cooley (Mordian); Len Hendry (Airport Attendant); Letty Light and Lucille Barkley (Salesgirls); Crane Whitley (Man with Cane); Michael Macey (Peasant); George Magrill, Carl Saxe, Tom Costello and George Bruggeman (Aides); Dorothy Barrett (Model in Window).

Signe Hasso and Hope in *Where There's Life* (1947).

Released November 21, 1947, by Paramount Pictures.

Where There's Life is one of the unfairly overlooked Hope comedies, perhaps because it came after four of the comedian's absolute best films: *The Princess and the Pirate, Road to Utopia, Monsieur Beaucaire,* and *My Favorite Brunette.* While it offers few surprises, *Where There's Life* is still a very funny movie.

When the ruler of a small country is killed, he reveals on his death bed that he has but one heir, a grandson. Michael Joseph Valentine (Hope), an American radio personality, is who he names. Valentine has no idea of this lineage; furthermore, he plans to end his womanizing ways and get married the following day. His fiancée (Vera Marshe) comes from a family of policemen, the most notorious being her brother Victor (William Bendix). While they're against the marriage, the family of cops is even more adamant that Valentine not back out of his promise. Valentine is kidnapped, escapes, attempts to get others to believe his story, and is continually beset by close calls, murders, and foiled attempts on his life.

Many of Hope's films have used a comic premise that involved spies, espionage, and murder, *My Favorite Blonde* and *They Got Me Covered* are two

Ad for *Where There's Life* (1947).

solid examples. *Where There's Life* is arguably every bit as fun and breezy as any similar Bob Hope feature.

As with most of Hope's films, the supporting cast is quite good. Signe Hasso began her film career at sixteen in her native Sweden before journeying to Hollywood in 1940. Perhaps her best work came the following year with *A Double Life*, but she does quite well in this Hope film as the lady general bent on delivering Valentine to her country.

William Bendix had been a successful character actor in dramas (*The Blue Dahlia*, *The Glass Key*) and comedies (Abbott and Costello's hilarious *Who Done It*), movie biographies (the notorious *Babe Ruth Story*) and screen adaptations of legitimate plays (the title role in Eugene O'Neill's *The Hairy Ape*). While filming *Where There's Life*, he was also appearing weekly on radio as Chester A. Riley in the popular series *The Life of Riley*. He would move the character to television in 1955 (a 1949 TV version of this same series starred Jackie Gleason, but despite winning an Emmy, it was canceled after one season).

Again, Hope is at his best when caught in a compromising situation. Whether he must explain the lady general's presence in his apartment to his fiancée or don a hood and pose as a member of his own execution team, his talent in these areas is clearly evident.

Hope also throws a few barbs at some usual targets. Upon sneaking through a duct system and into a room of hooded executioners, Hope looks around the room and mutters, "Democrats!" When he sees a poster advertising Bing Crosby's latest hit *Blue Skies*, he remarks to the lady general, "That's just a singer from before your time."

At the time of its initial release, *Where There's Life* was another big box office success. However, nowadays it is considered a good — not great — effort and a slight dip in quality from the four strong features by which it is preceded. This writer is willing to claim that *Where There's Life* makes five top-level Bob Hope films in a row.

Road to Rio

Directed by Norman Z. McLeod. Writing Credits: Edmund Beloin and Jack Rose. Produced by Daniel Dare. Original Music by Ary Barroso, Johnny Burke, Hannibal Cruz, Vicente Paiva, Luiz Peixoto, Sa Roris, Jimmy Van Heusen and Russo de Pandeiro. Cinematography by Ernest Laszlo. Film Editing by Ellsworth Hoagland. Art Direction by Hans Dreier and Earl Hedrick. Set Decoration by Sam Comer and Ray Moyer. Costume Design by Edith Head. Makeup by Wally Westmore. Assistant Director: Oscar Rudolph. Sound by Harold Lewis and Walter Oberst. Special Effects by Gordon Jennings, Paul K. Lerpae and Farciot Edouart. Choreography by Billy Daniel.

Cast: Bing Crosby (Scat Sweeney); Bob Hope (Hot Lips Barton); Dorothy Lamour (Lucia Maria de Andrade); Gale Sondergaard (Catherine Vail); Frank Faylen (Harry); Joseph Vitale (Tony); George Meeker (Sherman Malley); Frank Puglia (Rodrigues); Nestor Paiva (Cardoso); Robert Barrat (Johnson); Stanley Andrews (Captain Harmon); Harry Woods (Purser); Jerry Colonna (Cavalry Captain); Raul Roulien (Cavalry Officer); Frank Ferguson (Texas Posse Member); Stanley Blystone (Assistant Purser); George Chandler (Ship's Valet); Al Bridge (Ship's Officer); Arthur Q. Bryan (Mr. Stanton); George Sorel (The Prefecto); Martha Clemons (Bridesmaid); Laura Corbay (Specialty Dancer); Gino Corrado (The Barber); Ralph Dunn (Meat Delivery Foreman); Tor Johnson (Samson); Ralph Gomez, Duke York and Frank Hagney (Roustabout); Eddie Hall (Sideshow Audience Member); Brandon Hurst (Barker); Babe London (Woman); Donald Kerr (Steward); George Lloyd and Paul Newlan (Butchers); Charles Middleton (Farmer); William Newell (Meat Stamper); Patsy O'Byrne (Charwoman); Ray Teal (Buck); Tad Van Brunt (Pilot); Fred Zendar (Stevedore); Pepito Pérez (Dignified Gentleman); Barbara Pratt (Airline Hostess); Marquita Rivera (Lead Singer, Dancer); Harry Wiere, Herbert Wiere, Sylvester Wiere (The Wiere Brothers); Laverne Andrews, Maxene Andrews, Patty Andrews (The Andrews Sisters).

Released December 25, 1947, by Paramount Pictures.

Bing Crosby and Hope in *Road to Rio* (1947).

Just as *Where There's Life* is unfairly regarded as somewhat lesser than the Bob Hope features immediately preceding it, *Road to Rio* is often referred to as less interesting than Bing and Bob's treks to Morocco or Utopia. In fact, *Road to Rio* is another one of the funniest Road pictures.

Hope and Crosby play Scat Sweeney and Hot Lips Barton, two small-time musicians who inadvertently set fire to a circus big top where they are performing in a side show. They stow away on a ship bound for Rio where they discover the beautiful Lucia (Dorothy Lamour) attempting to commit suicide. She thanks them, but then she turns them over to the ship's captain. They soon discover that she has been hypnotized by her evil aunt and is soon to be forced into an unwanted marriage. The boys attempt to thwart the wedding plans.

It is interesting, at this point, to compare the Hope and Crosby relationship in this film to their first Road picture, *Road to Singapore*. In the first, Crosby has a wandering spirit and looks up to his pal Hope as a free-thinking rogue. By the time they made this film, Hope was established in films

Ad for *Road to Rio*, 1947.

as a back-pedaling coward. Crosby, then, was cast as the cool, calculating, manipulative friend who calls the shots and often dupes Hope into various schemes. Hope, in fact, will play the patsy who ends up in troublesome situations due to Crosby.

Road to Rio benefits from the presence of Gale Sondargaard as the conniving aunt who hypnotizes the hapless Lucia. Her ability to play cold, sinister parts such as this served her quite well throughout this leg of her career. She and her husband, director Abner Biberman, were blacklisted during the McCarthy witch hunts, and their careers were severely hampered. Sondergaard's career recovered and she was active in films and television until only a couple of years before her death in 1985, but the roles were far smaller than they had been.

One of the film's greatest highlights featured the Wiere Brothers as three musicians who do not speak English. The boys need to get them jobs in a nightclub and teach each of them only one phrase. The phrases are "This is murder," "You're telling me," and "You're in the groove, Jackson." This leads to a delightful bit with a frustrated club owner (Nestor Paiva).

The Wiere Brothers were successful vaudeville entertainers who did little work in films and on television. They did have a short-lived TV series in 1962, *Oh Those Bells*. *Road to Rio* may be their most-known work.

Another welcome addition to this Road picture is the Andrews Sisters, a popular singing act that had cut a few records with Bing. They are perhaps best known for their appearance in three Abbott and Costello movies (*Buck Privates, In the Navy,* and *Hold That Ghost*) as well as the hits "Boogie Woogie Bugle Boy" and "Apple Blossom Time."

Road to Rio is one of Hope and Crosby's funniest but is still generally considered to be below the high standard set by *Road to Utopia* and *Road to Morocco*. Bosley Crowther said this in his *New York Times* review:

> Fairly well loaded with laughs ... maybe not their funniest, but there are patches that contain their best work.

In fact, *Road to Rio* contains as many gags and as much fast-paced fun as any of the preceding Bob Hope classics, making the comedian's string of top comedy features an even half-dozen.

The Paleface

Directed by Norman Z. McLeod. Written by Edmund L. Hartmann and Frank Tashlin. Produced by Robert L. Welch. Original Music by Ray Evans, Jay Livingston, Victor Young and Joseph J. Lilley. Cinematography by Ray Rennahan. Film Editing by Ellsworth Hoagland. Art Direction by Hans Dreier and A. Earl Hedrick. Set Decoration by Sam Comer and Bertram C. Granger. Costume Design by Mary Kay Dodson. Makeup by Wally Westmore. Hair Stylists: Dean Cole and Lavaughn Speer. Production Manager: Charles Woolstenhulme. Sound by John Cope and Gene Merritt. Special Effects by Gordon Jennings. Stunt Double for Jane Russell: Sharon Lucas.

Cast: Bob Hope ("Painless" Peter Potter); Jane Russell (Calamity Jane); Robert Armstrong (Terris); Iris Adrian (Pepper); Bobby Watson (Toby Preston [as Robert Watson]); Jackie Searl (Jasper Martin [as Jack Searl]); Joseph Vitale (Indian Scout); Charles Trowbridge (Governor Johnson); Clem Bevans (Hank Billings); Jeff York (Big Joe); George Chandler (First Patient); Nestor Paiva (Second Patient); Stanley Andrews (Commissioner Emerson); Wade Crosby (Jeb); Chief Yowlachie (Chief Yellow Feather); Iron Eyes Cody (Chief Iron Eyes); Tom Kennedy (Bartender); Henry Brandon (Wapato, Medicine Man); Francis McDonald (Lance); Frank Hagney (Greg); Skelton Knaggs (Pete); Arthur Space (Zach); Charles Cooley (Mr. X); Eric Alden (Bob); Carl Andre, Ted Mapes and Kermit Maynard (Horsemen); Al Bridge and Trevor Bardette (Governor's Horsemen); Edgar Dearing (Sheriff); Dick Elliott (Mayor); Stanley Blystone (Saloon Patron Restraining Joe); Wally Boyle (Hotel Clerk); Paul E. Burns (Justice of the Peace); Hall Bartlett (Handsome Cowboy); Billy Engle (Pioneer); Laura Corbay and Margaret Field (Guests); Jody Gilbert (Woman in Bath House); John Maxwell (Village Gossip); Harry Harvey (Justice of the Peace); Al Hill (Pioneer); Earle Hodgins (Clem); Bob Kortman (Saloon Patron Restraining Joe); Ethan Laidlaw (Terris's Henchman); Dorothy Granger (Attendant at Bath House); Lane Chandler (Cowboy Advising "Lean to Right"); Syd Saylor (Cowboy Advising "Stand on Toes"); Oliver Blake (Cowboy Advising "Aim to West"); Olin Howlin (Jonathan Sloane, Undertaker); Houseley Stevenson (Pioneer); Loyal Underwood (Bearded

Character); Blackie Whiteford (Stagecoach Shotgun); Harry Wilson (Cowboy in Saloon); Duke York (Terris's Henchman); Babe London (Woman on Wagon Train); Marilyn Gladstone, June Glory, Dee La Nore, Betty Hannon, Maria J. Tavares and Charmienne Harker (B-Girls); Sharon McManus (Girl); John "Skins" Miller (Bellhop).

Released December 24, 1948, by Paramount Pictures.

After a string of a half-dozen of his best feature efforts, Bob Hope then appeared in what is, arguably, his greatest film of all. *The Paleface* is Hope's biggest moneymaking film and certainly one of the funniest comedy movies of its time.

Hope plays Painless Potter, a dentist in the Old West who uses laughing gas on his patients to obscure the pain. While working on patients, he gets mixed up with Calamity Jane. Jane is out to find who is selling guns to the Indians and is supposed to travel undercover with an agent, but when the agent is found dead, she enlists the unwitting Potter to travel with her. Potter is a coward but is embraced as a hero when, during an Indian attack, he proves himself to be an expert marksman. Little do the people of the wagon train, and Potter, realize, but it was Jane, hiding nearby, who killed all the Indians while Potter blindly shot toward the ground. Potter, however, gets to be full of himself and believes himself to be the hero that the townspeople think he is. Of course this doesn't bode well for the criminals who actually did sell weapons to the Indians. They also believe Potter to be a marksman and an agent and set out to do him in, not realizing he is no more than a cowardly dentist.

The Paleface was Bob Hope's biggest moneymaker and remains one of his very best films. A western setting was perfect for Hope's back-pedaling cowardly braggart. Perhaps due to the success of *The Paleface*, he was to revisit it a few more times.

In his very first scene, establishing Potter as an inept dentist who consults a textbook while working, Hope offers some solid comedy. Familiar character actor Nestor Paiva is a tough cowboy with a painful tooth. "When a tooth is no good you pull it!" he says. Potter checks the text, "Whaddya know, he's right!"

To live up to his painless tag, Potter applies laughing gas, causing himself and the patient to begin giggling. They remain giggling as he pulls the wrong tooth.

"I'm giving you just fifteen minutes to get out of town," laughs the patient. "Last town gave me twenty minutes!" laughs Potter.

Opposite page: Ad for *The Paleface*, 1948.

Potter's interest in the beautiful Calamity Jane (Jane Russell) is at such a level that he agrees to marry her and doesn't stop to realize he is being duped. She is using him merely as a decoy but ends up finding him endearing.

She quietly does the shooting and allows Potter to get the credit. He gathers the other members of the wagon train together to say a few words, whereupon one of the others shouts, "We better get going before more of those Indians come," and Potter replies, "Those are the words!" Still he becomes known as a cold-hearted killer who is merely posing as a dentist. "I wonder what the cowards are doing," he says, as he is greeted by awestruck townsfolk.

The criminals who are selling weapons to the Indians want Potter dead, so they arrange for him to be caught with a jealous cowboy's girl. "I don't like nobody foolin' around with my gal!" Potter, believing his own publicity states, "I'm not foolin!" This leads to an old-fashioned western duel.

As he prepares to go out and fight the duel, he is given suggestions by several. "He draws from the left, so lean to the right." "There's a wind from the east, better aim to the west." "He crouches when he shoots, so stand on your toes." Of course Potter confuses these tips, babbling, "He draws from the left, so stand on your toes." "He draws from his toes, so lean toward the wind." "He stands on his crouch, with his toes in the wind." "He draws from the west, so lean when you stand."

Jane plans to allow Potter to die in the gun battle, stating, "That takes care of that problem." However, she has come to find him endearing and shoots his adversary from a nearby building. Of course Potter gets the credit.

Another highlight has Potter captured by Indians and tied to two trees. When a rope is cut loose, the trees will spring up in opposite directions, tearing the victim in half. Potter, however, comes loose from one tree and is catapulted away. He dons Indian garb, infiltrates the tribe, and rescues Jane.

The Paleface is really quite similar to the spy and espionage comedies Hope made during the war, such as *My Favorite Blonde* and *They Got Me Covered*. In a western setting, the same type of undercover criminal activity is going on, Hope is the unwitting hero, and it is all for the sake of a woman who ends up falling for him at the end.

One of the best ingredients of *The Paleface* was the Oscar-nominated song, "Buttons and Bows," which became a big hit. It was the second song introduced by Hope to be nominated for an Academy Award, the first being "Thanks for the Memory" from *The Big Broadcast of 1938*.

While filming was about to commence on *The Paleface*, Hope took a trip to South America with his wife Dolores. During the boat trip home, Hope spent too much time sunning himself on deck and suffered from second-degree sunburn. He was hospitalized for two days, and filming had to be postponed for a week.

The Paleface is an outstanding Bob Hope comedy, benefiting from the wild comic vision of Frank Tashlin as well as the succession of one-liners provided by Hope's writers. Jane Russell, who became a sensation in the Howard Hughes production *The Outlaw*, gives an effectively deadpan performance as Jane. While the supporting cast includes such familiar actors as Robert Armstrong, Jackie Searl, and western movie stalwart Iron Eyes Cody, it is really Hope and Russell's show.

The massive success of *The Paleface* went beyond even Hope and Paramount's expectations. It grossed seven million dollars, which is amazing for 1948 when movie admission prices were in the area of twenty-five cents per ticket.

Sorrowful Jones

Directed by Sidney Lanfield. Screenplay by Edmund L. Hartmann, Jack Rose and Melville Shavelson. Story by Damon Runyon. Adapted by Sam Hellman, Gladys Lehman and William R. Lipman. Produced by Robert L. Welch. Original Music by Robert Emmett Dolan, Ray Evans and Jay Livingston. Cinematography by Daniel L. Fapp. Film Editing by Arthur P. Schmidt. Art Direction by Hans Dreier and Albert Nozaki. Set Decoration by Sam Comer and Bertram C. Granger. Costume Design by Mary Kay Dodson. Makeup by Wally Westmore. Assistant Director: Oscar Rudolph. Sound by John Cope and Harold Lewis. Special Effects by Gordon Jennings. Singing Voice for Lucille Ball: Annette Warren.

Cast: Bob Hope (Humphrey "Sorrowful" Jones); Lucille Ball (Gladys O'Neill); Mary Jane Saunders (Martha Jane Smith); William Demarest (Regret); Bruce Cabot (Big Steve Holloway); Thomas Gomez (Reardon); Tom Pedi (Once Over Sam); Paul Lees (Orville Smith); Houseley Stevenson (Doc Chesley); Ben Welden (Big Steve's Bodyguard); Emmett Vogan (Psychiatrist); Claire Carleton (Agnes "Happy Lips" Noonan); Sid Tomack (Waiter at Steve's Placer); Maurice Cass (Psychiatrist); Noble "Kid" Chissel (Bookie); Edgar Dearing (Police Lieutenant Mitchell); Charles Cooley (Shorty); Harry Tyler (Blinky); Joe Gray (Gambler); Arthur Space (Plainclothes Policeman); Louise Lorimer and Sally Rawlinson (Nurses); Selmer Jackson and John Shay (Doctors); John "Skins" Miller (Head Telephone Man); Marc Krah (Barber); Patsy O'Byrne (Scrubwoman); Ralph Peters (Taxicab Driver); Michael Cirillo, Tony Cirillo, James Cornell, James Davies, Sam Finn, Bob Kortman, Douglas Carter, John Mallon, Frank Mills, Allen Ray and Jack Roberts (Horse Players); William Yip, Pat Lane, Billy Snyder and Eddie Rio (Bookies); George Chan (Chinese Man); Orley Lindgren (bit part).

Released June 5, 1949, by Paramount Pictures.

It is interesting that Hope's tremendous success in films and continued success on radio were great enough to allow him to experiment in the fashion that he does with *Sorrowful Jones.*

Hope, William Demarest, Mary Jane Saunders and Lucille Ball in *Sorrowful Jones* (1949).

Most comedians of the post-war period in American movies experimented while maintaining their same comic image. The equally popular Abbott and Costello, for instance, felt the need to alter their inimitable style with two 1946 efforts: *Little Giant* (1946) and *Time of Their Lives* (1946). While it didn't alter their comic characters too much, each film featured the comedians in separate roles instead of as a team.

However, Hope decided to play it straight. While there are a handful of smart quips strewn about *Sorrowful Jones*, they appear to be more in keeping with the Damon Runyon world of streetwise sharpies. Hope's wisecracks are not as much jokes as a part of his character. While most of Hope's best films rely on his character's base cowardice in serious situations, this film features him in a much different role. *Sorrowful Jones* is a Runyonesque gambler with a heart of gold, although he doesn't realize his heart is so big until his cynical world is invaded by the innocence of an orphan child.

Sorrowful Jones is a remake of *Little Miss Marker*, which had been a hit for Shirley Temple in 1934. However, the film's name has been changed so that it is Hope who now plays the title character.

Sorrowful is a small-time bookmaker. One of his clients leaves his young daughter (Mary Jane Saunders) as security but is later killed. Sorrowful, then, is in a position where he feels he must look after the child.

As is typical with stories by Damon Runyon, there are many colorful characters. The most noted ones here are Gladys, played by Lucille Ball, and Regret, played by William Demarest.

Prior to becoming a television icon, Lucy tried her hand as an ingenue in lower-level RKO productions as well as straight dramatic roles in films like *Five Came Back* and *The Dark Corner*. She rarely had the opportunity to show off her comic skills before her landmark television series, but in *Sorrowful Jones* she does a good job of matching lines with Hope.

William Demarest was already a well-established character actor, never veering from his gruff persona in nearly one hundred and fifty feature films. Later audiences know him best as Uncle Charlie on the TV series *My Three Sons*. He took over the role after illness forced the retirement of William Frawley, of the *I Love Lucy* series, who had co-starred on *My Three Sons* as the grandfather, Bub O'Casey.

The highlight that is most often referred to in *Sorrowful Jones* is a tender moment between Sorrowful and the child. The child states that she doesn't believe in prayer or in God. Her father explained that there is no God. "When did he do that?" asks Sorrowful. "After my mother went away," she replies.

Sorrowful then tries to explain things to the innocent child. The little girl's impressionability and Hope's serious, pensive reaction make for one of the most moving sequences in the film. It is easy for a sequence such as this to appear maudlin, but Hope pulls it off quite nicely.

It is likely that Hope agreed to this more dramatic role in an attempt to appear more prestigious. It is an unfortunate truth that comedy is rarely recognized by such institutions as the Academy Awards, even though it is much more difficult to perform than drama. Hope's fine work as *Sorrowful Jones* does not negate the fact that he had already established himself as a wonderful comedian.

Hope thought he may have a shot at an Oscar nomination as Best Actor for *Sorrowful Jones*, realizing the Academy was notorious about overlooking the contributions of comedians. Unfortunately, Paramount failed to offer this film or Hope's performance for contention.

While different from the string of comedy hits that preceded it, *Sorrowful Jones* was another big box office success and was applauded by the critics.

The Great Lover

Directed by Alexander Hall. Writing Credits: Edmund Beloin, Melville Shavelson and Jack Rose. Produced by Edmund Beloin. Original Music by Ray Evans, Joseph J. Lilley, Jay Livingston, Edward H. Plumb and Roy Webb. Cinematography by Charles Lang. Film Editing by Ellsworth Hoagland. Art Direction by Hans Dreier and A. Earl Hedrick. Set Decoration by Sam Comer and Ross Dowd. Costume Design by Edith Head. Makeup by Wally Westmore, Charles Berner and Karl Silvera. Assistant Director: John R. Coonan. Sound Department: Harold Lewis and Walter Oberst. Special Effects by Farciot Edouart and Gordon Jennings.

Cast: Bob Hope (Freddie Hunter); Rhonda Fleming (Duchess Alexandria); Roland Young (C. J. Dabney); Roland Culver (Grand Duke Maximillian); George Reeves (Williams); Jim Backus (Higgins); Richard Lyon (Stanley Wilson); Gary Gray (Tommy O'Connor); Jerry Hunter (Herbie); Jackie Jackson (Joe); Karl Wright Esser (Steve); Orley Lindgren (Bill); Curtis Loys Jackson, Jr. (Humphrey); Sig Arno (Attendant); Albin Robeling (Waiter); Chester Clute (Man Drinking in Cabin); Jack Benny (Cameo Appearance).

Released November 23, 1949, by Paramount Pictures.

It is this writer's contention that *The Great Lover* is a lesser effort for Bob Hope. This, however, is not a popular opinion. Leonard Maltin gave three stars out of four to *The Great Lover* in his book, *TV Movies*. Woody Allen has cited *The Great Lover* as one of his favorite Hope films. Allen admits that, as with all of Hope's films, it is not the stuff of great cinema, but he cites *The Great Lover* as a strong inspiration for his own *Manhattan Murder Mystery*.

Hope plays Freddie, a scoutmaster traveling with his troop on a liner that is also carrying a murderous gambler. A private eye is after the killer, while Freddie has designs on a beautiful duchess who believes him to be a wealthy American traveler.

Freddie is a wisecracking newspaper man who volunteered to chaper-

Hope and Rhonda Fleming in *The Great Lover* (1949).

one the Boy Forresters upon their winning a trip to Paris. However, Freddie's intentions were hardly in line with the Forrester motto:

"I spent two weeks on a bicycle seat. I'd wake up peddling!

A Boy Forrester doesn't smoke, doesn't drink — he doesn't!"

At one point, the leader of the boys reminds Freddie that a Forrester doesn't make mistakes. "It's too bad your parents weren't Forresters," Freddie quips.

Once they have boarded the ocean liner, Freddie plans on sneaking off the boat and returning to Paris with an address book he won at a raffle held at the American Legion. When he bumps into the beautiful Duchess Alexandria (Rhonda Fleming), he decides to remain on the boat.

The duchess is traveling with her father, the Grand Duke Maximillian, (Roland Culver), who is noted as one of the wealthiest men in the world but who is now nearly broke and is traveling to America in an attempt to rebuild his fortune.

Roland Young plays Dabney, the murderous card sharp out to win the money he believes the Duke to still have. The duchess woos Freddie, whom she believes to be a wealthy American. Freddie tries to make time with the duchess while the scouts are watching his every move, and a private detective (Jim Backus) is on the trail of the killer.

Many of the scenes between Hope and the boys are among the film's few highlights.

SCOUT LEADER: Will you be cheerful, truthful, brave and clean?
FREDDIE: I'll be brave and clean
SCOUT LEADER: No tobacco or alcohol?
FREDDIE: No tobacco or alcohol.
SCOUT LEADER: No women?
FREDDIE: No tobacco.

The scout leader angrily turns to walk away, whereupon Freddie amends his previous answer.

Ad for *The Great Lover*, 1949.

FREDDIE: OK, no women — over sixty.

The only reason Freddie bothers listening to the scouts at all is because the troop leader's father is the owner of the newspaper on which Freddie is employed. For their part, the scouts believe it is their mission to save Freddie from his weaknesses, as is their motto.

SCOUT: Why couldn't Freddie be chaperone to the Campfire Girls?
SCOUT LEADER: Don't think he wouldn't like to!

Perhaps an entire film about Freddie's two weeks in Paris being dogged by upstanding Boy Forresters would have been a more amusing premise than the one featured in *The Great Lover*. The pace is slower, more like a mystery than a comedy-mystery. The situations take longer to build. The sequences with the scouts don't blend well with the slow-moving murder mystery. Scenes between Hope and Fleming lack the chemistry that flowed so effortlessly from Hope and his other female co-stars. Scenes like Freddie trying to thread a needle while the Duchess snuggles with him flirtatiously are only mildly amusing but are among the film's few real comedy sequences. Even the characteristic one-liners seem to be at a minimum.

Murder-mystery combined with comedy worked well for Hope, especially in *My Favorite Brunette*, which is one of his best films. However, while *My Favorite Brunette* managed to maintain a solid mystery while still presenting some very funny comedy, *The Great Lover* seems pallid by comparison.

Perhaps the most interesting aspect of *The Great Lover* is that in only five minutes of screen time, George Reeves, later TV's Superman, registers well as the murderer's first victim.

Fancy Pants

Directed by George Marshall. Writing Credits: Edmund L. Hartmann and Robert O'Brien. Original Story "Ruggles of Red Gap" by Harry Leon Wilson. Produced by Robert L. Welch. Original Music by Ray Evans, Jay Livingston and Van Cleave. Cinematography by Charles Lang. Film Editing by Archie Marshek. Art Direction by Hans Dreier and A. Earl Hedrick. Set Decoration by Sam Comer and Emile Kuri. Costume Design by Mary Kay Dodson and Gile Steele. Makeup Department: Charles Berner, Karl Silvera and Wally Westmore. Assistant Director: Oscar Rudolph. Sound by Don Johnson and Gene Merritt. Special Effects by Farciot Edouart and Gordon Jennings. Singing Voice for Lucille Ball: Annette Warren.

Cast: Bob Hope (Arthur Tyler); Lucille Ball (Agatha Floud); Bruce Cabot (Cart Belknap); Jack Kirkwood (Mike Floud); Lea Penman (Effie Floud); Hugh French (George Van-Basingwell); Eric Blore (Sir Wimbley); Joseph Vitale (Wampum); John Alexander (Teddy Roosevelt); Charles Cooley (Parson); Virginia Keiley (Rosalind); Colin Keith-Johnston (Twombley); Norma Varden (Lady Maude); Robin Hughes (Cyril); Hope Sansberry (Millie); Almira Sessions (Belle); Ida Moore (Bessie and Betsy); Grace Gillern Albertson (Dolly); Alva Marie Lacy (Daisy); Jean Ruth (Miss Wilkins); Ethel Wales (Mrs. Wilkins); Percy Helton (Mayor Fogarty); Hank Bell (Barfly); Ray Bennett (Secret Service Man); Oliver Blake (Mr. Andrews); Chester Conklin (Guest); Edgar Dearing (Mr. Jones); Joey Wong (Wong); Alex Frazer (Stagehand); Jimmie Dundee (Henchman); Sam Harris (Umpire); Olaf Hytten (Stage Manager); Bob Kortman (Henchman); Harry Martin (Englishman); Howard Petrie (Secret Service Man); Gilchrist Stuart (Wicket Keeper); Vincent Garcia, Gilbert Alonzo, David Alvarado, Robert Dominguez, Alfred Nunez and Henry Mirelez (Indian Boys).

Released July 15, 1950, by Paramount Pictures.

Fancy Pants is a remake of the 1935 classic *Ruggles of Red Gap* and suffers in the translation. While it works fairly well as a Hope picture, it does not

Ad for *Fancy Pants*, 1950.

hold up to the original, which featured Charles Laughton as a stuffy English manservant who is lost by his master in a poker game and must travel to a rustic American town.

In the remake, Hope is actor Arthur Tyler, stranded in the Wild West, who must pose as the butler for the loud, abrasive Agatha Cloud (Lucille Ball). Much of the comedy deals with Arthur's attempt to deal with the uncouth ways of the western types, especially tough guy Bruce Cabot who has designs on Agatha. Eventually, Arthur is mistaken for an earl and must represent himself when Theodore Roosevelt is scheduled to make a visit to the town.

Fancy Pants moves rather slowly and has only a few amusing scenes. Perhaps the funniest part of the picture actually occurs during the credits. Hope's face fills the screen and he states, derisively, "No popcorn during my performance. Peasants!"

Hope himself was unenthused with *Fancy Pants*. After seeing a rough cut, Hope insisted on reshooting some of the scenes that dragged and planned to work with his writers on some better material. However, shortly after deciding this, he was involved in a car accident and was unable to complete the retakes. Hope was to fully recover from the car accident. *Fancy Pants*, however, never recovered.

The Lemon Drop Kid

Directed by Sidney Lanfield and Frank Tashlin. Writing Credits: Edmund Beloin, Irving Elinson, Edmund L. Hartmann, Robert O'Brien, Damon Runyon and Frank Tashlin. Produced by Robert L. Welch. Original Music by Ray Evans, Jay Livingston and Victor Young. Cinematography by Daniel L. Fapp. Film Editing by Archie Marshek. Art Direction by Franz Bachelin and Hal Pereira. Set Decoration by Sam Comer and Ross Dowd. Costume Design by Edith Head. Makeup by Wally Westmore. Sound by Don McKay and Walter Oberst. Special Effects by Farciot Edouart.

Cast: Bob Hope (Sidney Melbourne [The Lemon Drop Kid]); Marilyn Maxwell ("Brainy" Baxter); Lloyd Nolan (Oxford Charlie); Jane Darwell (Nellie Thursday); Andrea King (Stella); Fred Clark (Moose Moran); Jay C. Flippen (Straight Flush); William Frawley (Gloomy Willie); Harry Bellaver (Sam the Surgeon); Sid Melton (Little Louie); Ben Welden (Singing Solly); Ida Moore (The Bird Lady); Francis Pierlot (Henry Regan); Charles Cooley (Goomba); Salvatore De Lorenzo (Street Corner Santa Claus [as Society Kid Hogan]); Harry Shannon (John, the Policeman); Helen Brown (Ellen); Bernard Szold (Honest Harry); Tor Johnson (Super Swedish Angel, the Wrestler); Tom Dugan (No Thumbs Charlie); Slim Gaut (Professor Murdock); Stanley Andrews (Judge); Almira Sessions (Mrs. Santoro); Tommy Ivo (Boy Scout); Fred Zendar (South Street Benny); Fred Graff (Pimlico Pete); Jim Haywood (George); Richard Karlan (Maxie); Ray Cooke (Willie); Gene Roth (Oxford Charlie's Henchman); Jack Kruschen and John Doucette (Musclemen); Harry Tyler (Santa Claus); Roy Gordon (Judge); Jean Whitney (Friend of Brainy); Douglas Spencer (Skinny Santa Claus); Sid Tomack (Groom); Ralph Dunn (Race Track Policeman); Bill Varga (Wrestler); Mary Murphy (Girl); Vivian Mason (Singer-Dancer); Bill Sheehan (Dance Director).

Released March 8, 1951, by Paramount Pictures.

Bob Hope portrays Sidney Melbourne, a Runyonesque racetrack tout

Opposite page: Ad for *The Lemon Drop Kid*, 1951.

BOB HOPE's THREE TIMES FUNNIER

Bob's a scream as his own charming aunt!

...with all the zany guys and gals of Damon Runyon's beloved masterpiece!

Bob's a riot as Santa!

When Bob takes over the Santa Claus concession... it's the funniest thing south of the North Pole!

Bob's a howl as a Broadway character!

Hope's hiding behind a lady's skirt... but this time it's his own!

NELLIE THURSDAY

OXFORD CHARLIE

STELLA GORMAN

MOOSE MORAN

BRAINY BAXTER

Damon Runyon's
The LEMON DROP KID

All the wonderful Damon Runyon guys and gals join in the big "Silver Bells" number!

SILVER BELLS

YOU'LL HEAR

"Silver Bells"

"They Obviously Want Me To Sing"

"It Doesn't Cost A Dime To Dream"

A Paramount Picture starring

Bob Hope

Marilyn Maxwell · Lloyd Nolan · Jane Darwell

with ANDREA KING · FRED CLARK · HARRY BELLAVER Produced by ROBERT L. WELCH
Directed by SIDNEY LANFIELD · Screenplay by Edmund Hartmann, Robert O'Brien and Frank Tashlin · Additional Dialogue by Irving Elinson · Story by Edmund Beloin · Based on Damon Runyon's "The Lemon Drop Kid"
You'll see such characters as: SAM THE SURGEON · SINGIN' SOLLY · GOOMBA · STRAIGHT FLUSH · GLOOMY WILLIE · LITTLE LOUIE

with an affinity for lemon drops. He gets into hot water with a local crime boss (Lloyd Nolan), owing him $10,000. Sidney has until Christmas to make the payoff.

Sidney comes upon a scheme to raise the money. He tells his girlfriend (Marilyn Maxwell) and assorted friends that he wants to raise money for a senior citizen's center. They all don Santa Claus outfits and collect money throughout New York City.

Sidney plans to use the donations to pay off his debt. However, a rival gang lord reveals Sidney's scheme and takes over the Santa racket himself. Sidney, having a change of heart after seeing the happiness the old women are enjoying in their new center, redeems himself by trapping both crime bosses, making sure the senior citizen home gets the donations.

As the Runyon stories are filled with colorful characters, *The Lemon Drop Kid* features many top character actors, including William Frawley, Jay C. Flippen, Ben Welden, and Sid Melton, all of whom fit nicely into the Runyonesque framework.

Something of a Christmas perennial with an uplifting holiday message, *The Lemon Drop Kid* is one of the more pleasant Hope comedies. Its major highlight is the song, "Silver Bells," which became a staple of Hope's Christmas specials for many decades.

However "Silver Bells" was not originally in the film. Hope saw a rough cut of *The Lemon Drop Kid* and was not pleased. In fact, he refused to let Barney Balaban, Paramount studio head, release the film for the Christmas season until several scenes were re-shot.

In his book *The Road to Hollywood*, Hope recalled a conversation with Balaban shortly after the completion of *The Lemon Drop Kid*:

> (Barney and I) went to the Beverly Hills Hotel for a drink and I argued that the picture could profit from some additions. I must have argued pretty well because Paramount went back for retakes that cost $200,000. Frank Tashlin, whose wacky humor I admired, was assigned to do a rewrite. He ran the picture, together with a recording of the laughs from the preview. Then he put blank film in the picture where he planned additions. Frank showed me *The Lemon Drop Kid* that way, explaining what would be added to the blank scenes. "I'll do the rewrite," Frank said, "if you let me direct it." We agreed and that is how Tashlin became a director.

The entire climax was rewritten and directed by Frank Tashlin.

Also added was the song, "Silver Bells," penned by Livingston and Evans, who had written the popular "Buttons and Bows" for *The Paleface*. Both were among the highlights of the film, so Hope's instincts were correct, especially in hiring Tashlin to complete the retakes. "Silver Bells," in fact, has sold over thirty-two million records and nearly two million copies of sheet music.

Strangely, the song "Silver Bells" was originally titled "Tinkle Bells." It was Jay Livingston's wife who informed him that the word "tinkle" often stood for something else.

While the retakes were being arranged, Hope also had to begin the next season of his radio show and was once again entertaining the troops. America became involved in the Korean conflict, so Hope took an entertainment troupe to Korea, having the rough time of entertaining GI's in outdoor theaters during midwinter. It was, however, worthwhile to Hope, who often expressed his satisfaction at hearing the carefree laughter of men who were about to go to war.

Among Hope's writers on this trip to Korea was Larry Gelbart, who later created and wrote the popular TV series *M*A*S*H*, based on the Robert Altman film about the Korean war. The series ran nine years, six years longer than the actual war.

My Favorite Spy

Directed by Norman Z. McLeod. Written by Edmund Beloin, Lou Breslow, Edmund L. Hartmann, Jack Sher and Hal Kanter. Produced by Paul Jones. Original Music by Victor Young, Robert Emmett Dolan, Jay Livingston, Ray Evans and Johnny Mercer. Cinematography by Victor Milner. Film Editing by Frank Bracht. Art Direction by Roland Anderson and Hal Pereira. Set Decoration by Sam Comer and Grace Gregory. Costume Design by Edith Head. Makeup Department: Wally Westmore. Sound by Gene Merritt. Special Effects by Gordon Jennings and Farciot Edouart.

Cast: Bob Hope (Peanuts White/Eric Augustine); Hedy Lamarr (Lily Dalbray); Francis L. Sullivan (Karl Brubaker); Arnold Moss (Tasso); John Archer (Henderson); Luis Van Rooten (Rudolf Hoenig); Alden "Stephen" Chase (Donald Bailey); Morris Ankrum (General Frazer); Angela Clarke (Gypsy Fortune Teller); Iris Adrian (Lola); Frank Faylen (Newton); Mike Mazurki (Monkara); Marc Lawrence (Ben Ali); Tonio Selwart (Harry Crock); Ralph Smiley (El Sarif); Monique Chantal (Denise); Joseph Vitale (Fireman); Nestor Paiva (Fire Chief); Chester Conklin, Hank Mann and Billy Engle (Short Comics); Lyle Moraine (Foster); Helen Chapman (Miss Dieckers); Michael Ansara and Don Dunning (House Servants); Charles D. Campbell (Hatter); Fritz Feld (Dress Designer); Mike Mahoney (Murphy); Sayre Dearing (Casino Dealer); Roy Roberts (Johnson); Kasey Rogers (Maria); Alvina Temple (Miss Murphy); Ralph Montgomery (Grant); Ed Agresti (Tangier Policeman); Stanley Blystone (Guard); Eugene Borden (Manager); Veola Vonn (Tara); Crane Whitley (Willie); Roy Butler (Barber); Ralph Byrd (Official); Jack Chefe and Michael Cirillo (Waiters); Carlos Conde (Porter); Abdullah Abbas (Fireman/Egyptian porter); Delmar Costello (Beggar); Roger Creed (Photo Double); Gay Gayle (Flower Seller); Frank Hagney (Camel-herd); Bobby Hall (Tailor); Pepe Hern (Bellboy); F. Herrick Herrick, Jerry James, Jimmie Dundee, Lee Bennett and Jack Pepper (FBI Men); William Johnstone (Prentice); Norbert Schiller (Dr. Estrallo); George Lynn (Official); Myron Marks (Doorman); Alphonse Martell (French Assistant Manager); Patti McKay (Dancer); Torben Meyer (Headwaiter); Steven Geray and Jean De Briac (Croupiers);

Suzanne Dalbert (Barefoot Maid); Henry Mirelez and Tony Mirelez (Shine Boys); Geraldine Knapp (Maid with Towels); Mary Murphy (Manicurist); Alberto Morin (Hotel Employee); Dario Piazza (Waiter); Rudy Rama (Knife Man); Howard Negley (Guard); Paul Newlan and Michael Ross (Tangier Policemen); Ralph Sanford (Burlesque Husband); Alfredo Santos (Servant); Rolfe Sedan (Waiter); Marie Thomas (Cafe Patron); Ivan Triesault (Gunman); Felipe Turich (Porter); Loyal Underwood (Beggar); John Tegner (Judo Teacher); Joan Whitney (Blonde in Bathtub); Nancy Duke, Mimi Berry, Mary Ellen Gleason, Edith Sheets, Leah Waggner and Carolyn Wolfson (Girls in Casino); Duke York (Man); Pat Moran (Little Man); Lillian Molieri (Girl); Sue Casey and Dorothy Abbott (Pretty Girls); Suzanne Ridgeway, Charlotte Hunter, Peggy Gordon and Sethma Williams (Dancers).

Released December 25, 1951, by Paramount Pictures.

This time Hope plays Peanuts White, a burlesque comic who is recruited by U.S. agents to impersonate his double, Eric Augustine, an international spy. He must secure a million-dollar microfilm from a remote area of Tangiers. There, he hooks up with Augustine's girl, Lily Dalbray (Hedy Lamarr), who is now with his arch-enemy, Brubaker (Francis L. Sullivan).

Another Hope film revolving around international spies is perfectly enjoyable but also indicates something of a rut for Bob Hope's films. They were generally fresh and enjoyable from 1941 until the end of the decade, but as the 1950s approached they settled into a comfortable niche that threatened to become tiresome.

While *My Favorite Spy* is a good, solid comedy, it offers no real surprises other than a wild slapstick chase sequence that was expertly directed by Frank Tashlin.

The cast is filled with solid actors who have appeared in classic film noir, but despite occasional homages to films like *The Maltese Falcon*, *My Favorite Spy* is no more than an amusing, competent comedy.

Of course it can be argued that Hope's niche was what made his films of this period so successful and beloved by audiences. Even the critics remained amused at this point. As post-war America was once again sending soldiers overseas for battle, a period of dull, cultural conservatism settled in. While filmmakers like Alfred Hitchcock chose to peer into what evils may lurk behind the locked doors of American life (as with the brilliant 1954 film *Rear Window*), many filmmakers were content to churn out safe, predictable comedies that offered no challenge. *My Favorite Spy* is a good example.

Removed from the context of its period, *My Favorite Spy* is an enjoyable funny movie that will sufficiently amuse television viewers on a Sunday afternoon. However, within the overall context of Hope's movie career, it

Frank Toshlin discusses the next scene with Hope and Hedy Lamarr in *My Favorite Spy* (1951).

was evident that the comedian had reached a point where he had settled into an all too predictable pattern.

Many comedians who had been popular during the war years had the same problem. Abbott and Costello's films of the 1950s were hit-or-miss, as their fast-paced antics often slowed into tiresome rehashes of past successes. While there were some good Abbott and Costello movies made during the 1950s, their heyday was behind them (for a time during the 1940s, Abbott and Costello were the most popular film stars in the country).

My Favorite Spy is indicative of Hope's need for new material or, at the very least, a fresher approach to his formula.

Son of Paleface

Directed by Frank Tashlin. Written by Joseph Quillan, Frank Tashlin and Robert L. Welch. Produced by Robert L. Welch. Original Music by Jack Brooks and Lyn Murray. Non-Original Music by Ray Evans and Jay Livingston (Song: "Buttons and Bows"). Cinematography by Harry J. Wild. Film Editing by Eda Warren. Art Direction by Roland Anderson and Hal Pereira. Special Effects by Farciot Edouart, Gordon Jennings, Paul K. Lerpae and Josephine Earl.

Cast: Bob Hope (Junior Potter); Jane Russell (Mike Delroy aka The Torch); Roy Rogers (Roy Barton); Bill Williams (Kirk); Lloyd Corrigan (Doc Lovejoy); Paul E. Burns (Ebenezer Hawkins); Douglass Dumbrille (Sheriff McIntyre); Harry von Zell (Mr. Stoner the Banker); Iron Eyes Cody (Chief Yellow Cloud); William "Wee Willie" Davis (Blacksmith); Charles Cooley (Charley); Jean Willes (Penelope, Jr.'s Girl at Harvard); Frank Cordell (Dade); William Willingham (Jeb); Isabel Cushin (Isabel); Lyle Moraine (Waverly, Bank Clerk); Felice Richmond (Genevieve); Don Dunning (Wally); Jane Easton (Clara); Warren Fiske (Trav); John George (Johnny); Jonathan Hale (Gov. Freeman); Charmienne Harker (Bessie); Charles Morton (Ned); Leo J. McMahon (Craig); Flo Stanton (Flo); Charles Quirk (Zeke); Oliver Blake (Telegrapher); Homer Dickenson (Townfolk); Anne Dore (She-Devil); Michael Cirillo (Indian); Jack Pepper (Customer in Restaurant); Hank Mann (First Bartender); Chester Conklin (Second Bartender); Cecil B. DeMille and Bing Crosby (Cameo Appearances); Robert L. Welch (Cameo Appearance as DeMille's Assistant).

Released July 14, 1952, by Paramount Pictures.

Having sunk into something of a rut with many of his past few pictures, Hope needed a creative shot in the arm as far as his movie career was concerned. The films were still popular and scored big at the box office, keeping Hope among the top box office stars in America, but they had settled into a niche that was a bit too comfortable and was becoming predictable.

Son of Paleface is, of course, a sequel to *The Paleface*. It is also Hope's best film since that 1948 classic and one of the best of his entire career.

Many critics, including Leonard Maltin, Pauline Kael, and Dave Kehr, believe this Frank Tashlin film to be superior to the original, much as *Godfather II* is a better film than *The Godfather*. It is also, however, important to remember that *The Godfather* still remains one of the best films of its kind, despite the superior sequel.

Son of Paleface deals with the life of the pampered Junior Potter, the son of Painless. The lad has enjoyed the sheltered existence of the wealthy and is a Harvard graduate who travels to the Old West where his father was noted as an Indian fighter.

Junior is interested in claiming the inheritance left by his father. He gets mixed up with a beautiful woman (Jane Russell) who is thought to be stealing gold shipments and a cowboy (Roy Rogers) who has set out to capture the bandits stealing the gold.

This was Frank Tashlin's script and the first film for which he is credited as sole director. His background writing animated cartoons for Warner Brothers gave him a certain surreal outlook on how to present comedy. The humor in *Son of Paleface* is often very wild, especially the final chase sequence. Chase endings were a staple of many Tashlin-directed films, including *Kill the Umpire* and *The Disorderly Orderly*, among others. His surreal visual concept was a hit with French auteur critics like Jean Luc Godard and François Truffaut and was a strong influence on Jerry Lewis's films as a director.

Tashlin's other forte was satire, as can be seen with his amusing attacks on show biz glitz (*Will Success Spoil Rock Hunter*) and rock and roll (*The Girl Can't Help It*).

Along with the wild comedy, *Son of Paleface* succeeds as a western send-up. Even the casting of clean-cut cowboy superstar Roy Rogers, essentially appearing as himself, is inspired.

At this time, Rogers had been an enormous star for nearly a decade and the idol of millions of children. An actual cowboy offscreen, and not merely an actor or businessman like Gene Autry and many of his other contemporaries, Rogers adds authenticity to Tashlin's lampoon of the genre.

In one sequence, Rogers is asked if he likes girls. "I'll stick to horses," is his straight-faced reply.

One of the major reasons for Rogers's popularity was his horse, Trigger, known as "The Smartest Horse in Movies." One of the film's highlights features Junior having to sleep in the same bed as the animal. The two of them keep fighting over the blankets. First Junior takes them from the horse and lies down. Then the horses reaches over and pulls them back with his teeth. Trigger manages to match Hope's timing.

During the final chase sequence, Tashlin's penchant for surreal cartoon-like gags really comes forward. At one point, the car in which Junior is riding loses a wheel. From inside the car, he lassoes the axle and holds the car up as Rogers rides ahead to get the wheel. "Hurry up," cries Junior, "this is impossible!"

"Buttons and Bows," the award-nominated song from the original film, is reintroduced here. Roy Rogers and Jane Russell sing, while Hope chimes in with amusing asides.

This was one of the last films Rogers made. (He did a brief cameo in another Hope film several years later and made a comeback film, *Mackintosh and T. J.*, a few decades down the road). By now, Rogers was completely established in film, so he decided to relax with a television series and manage his hundred million dollars worth of real estate holdings. His lampoon in *Son of Paleface* seems a perfect culmination to his career. Until his death in 1999, Rogers would always cite *Son of Paleface* as among the most enjoyable experiences he'd had in movies.

Son of Paleface was a huge box office success, but Hope's films always made money. The difference is that this was more than merely an amusing formula effort. It is one of the five-or-so best Bob Hope movies overall.

Road to Bali

Directed by Hal Walker. Writing Credits: Frank Butler, Hal Kanter and William Morrow. Story by Harry Tugend. Produced by Daniel Dare and Harry Tugend. Original Music by Johnny Burke, Joseph J. Lilley, Jimmy Van Heusen, Gerard Carbonara, Stan Kenton, Gus Levene, Pete Rugolo, Leo Shuken and Van Cleave. Cinematography by George Barnes. Film Editing by Archie Marshek. Art Direction by J. McMillan Johnson and Hal Pereira. Set Decoration by Sam Comer and Ross Dowd. Costume Design by Edith Head. Makeup by Wally Westmore. Sound by John Cope and Gene Merritt. Choreography by Charles O'Curran.

Cast: Bing Crosby (George Cochran); Bob Hope (Harold Gridley); Dorothy Lamour (Princess Lala); Murvyn Vye (Ken Arok); Peter Coe (Gung); Ralph Moody (Bhoma Da); Leon Askin (Ramayana); Bernie Gozier (Bo Kassar); Carolyn Jones (Eunice); Jan Kayne (Verna); Douglas Yorke (Verna's Brother); Allan Nixon (Eunice's Brother); Roy Gordon (Eunice's Father); Harry Cording (Verna's Father); Bunny Lewbel (Lala Age Seven); Michael Ansara (Guard); Herman Cantor (Priest); Donald Lawton (Employment Agent); Larry Chance (Attendant); Richard Keene (Conductor); Mary Kanae (Old Crone); Kukhie Kuhns (Fat Woman in Basket); My Lee Haulani (Beautiful Girl in Basket); Sue Casey, Leslie Charles, Patricia Dane, Judith London, Patti McKay, Betty Onge and Jean Corbett (Handmaidens); Satini Pualoa, Charles Mauu, Kuka T. Tuitama and Al Kikume (Warriors); Raymond Lee and Luukia Luana (Boys); Ethel K. Reiman, Irene K. Silva and Shela Fritz (Chief's Wives); Bhogwan Singh, Besmark Auelua, Chanan Singh Sohi and Jerry Groves (Lesser Priests); Bob Crosby (himself); Jane Russell (Cameo Appearance); Dean Martin and Jerry Lewis (Men in Lala's Dream); Humphrey Bogart and Katharine Hepburn (In Footage from African Queen); Jack Claus (Specialty Dancer).

Released November 19, 1952, by Paramount Pictures.

Road to Bali is the sixth Road picture and the only one in color. Hope and Crosby are vaudevillians in Australia who are once again forced to leave town after breaking the hearts of some maidens with angry fathers. They land jobs as divers and end up in the South Seas, where an appropriately sarong-clad Dorothy Lamour appears as a rich islander.

Twelve years after the first Road picture, Bing and Bob seem to be taking it all in stride. The jokes are there and so is a reasonable amount of enthusiasm, but too much of *Road to Bali* relies on novelty.

There are some fun cameos of Jane Russell, Dean Martin and Jerry Lewis, Katharine Hepburn, and Humphrey Bogart. However, these are inserted without any real setup, merely as window dressing for a film that doesn't try to stand alone.

Perhaps the funniest cameo comes from Bing's brother, bandleader Bob Crosby, who walks up to the duo, fires off a gun in the air, and leaves. Bing quips, "I promised my brother Bob a shot in the picture."

Road to Bali still has an appropriately breezy pace and amusing jokes, but it is probably the weakest Road picture thus far.

Perhaps the most interesting thing about this film is that during its shooting, Hope and Crosby stopped in on the set of Cecil B. DeMille's *The Greatest Show on Earth* to do a brief, unbilled cameo as members of the audience.

Off Limits

Directed by George Marshall. Story and screenplay by Hal Kanter and Jack Sher. Produced by Harry Tugend. Original Music by Ray Evans, Jay Livingston and Van Cleave. Cinematography by J. Peverell Marley. Film Editing by Arthur P. Schmidt. Art Direction by Hal Pereira and Walter H. Tyler. Set Decoration by Sam Comer and Grace Gregory. Costume Design by Edith Head. Makeup by Wally Westmore. Special Effects by Farciot Edouart and Gordon Jennings.

Cast: Bob Hope (Wally Hogan); Mickey Rooney (Herbert Tuttle); Marilyn Maxwell (Connie Curtis); Eddie Mayehoff (Karl Danzig); Stanley Clements (Bullets Bradley); Jack Dempsey (Jack Dempsey); Marvin Miller (Vic Breck); John Ridgely (Lieutenant Commander Parnell); Carolyn Jones (Deborah); Norman Leavitt (Chowhound); Joan Taylor (Helen); Jerry Hausner (Fishy); Billy Nelson (Polaski); Mike Mahoney (M. P. Huggins); Kim Spalding (Seaman Harker); Tom Dugan (Bartender); Mary Murphy (WAC Soldier); James Seay (Doctor); Art Aragon and Tom Harmon (themselves).

Released February 15, 1953, by Paramount Pictures.

Boxing is a staple in comedy.

There are boxing sequences featuring Chaplin (*City Lights*), Laurel and Hardy (*The Battle of the Century, Any Old Port*), and Abbott and Costello (*Buck Privates*).

Several comedies concentrate on a boxing theme, from the Snub Pollard silent *Looking for Trouble* or the Three Stooges short *Punch Drunks*, to Joe E. Brown in *When's Your Birthday* and Buster Keaton's *Battling Butler*.

Hope was not the type of comedian to play a boxer, although he had been one as a youth. He is perfectly cast, however, as a glib boxing manager.

Hope is Wally Hogan, a fight manager who successfully trains the protégé of gangsters into a champion. When the fighter (Stanley Clements) is drafted, Wally is expected to go along and keep training him. However, when

Ad for *Off Limits*, 1953.

the fighter is declared 4F, Wally is stuck in the army, discovering the whole thing was a scam by the gangsters to get him out of the way.

Hogan befriends another soldier (Mickey Rooney), who longs to be a fighter despite opposition from his aunt (Marilyn Maxwell), who deplores violence. Hope takes Rooney under his wing and Rooney eventually has a championship fight with Hogan's former protégé.

Mickey Rooney had spent the late 1930s and early 1940s as one of the hottest box office attractions for MGM. When the war ended, bad business and personal decisions resulted in his star plummeting rapidly. By 1953 he was considered a has-been by the industry. Hope was among the few who still believed in Rooney and was instrumental in Mickey being signed for *Off Limits*.

In his book *The Road to Hollywood*, Hope recalled:

> Paramount had some doubts about hiring Mickey for the role. He had a reputation for liking the nightclub life, and the studio was worried that he might not prove reliable. I said, "Mickey is one of the most talented actors in this town." As I expected, Mickey was totally professional throughout the shooting. When *Off Limits* was released, the critics raved about the combination of Hope and Rooney.

In an interview with this writer, Rooney stated,

> I was a star. For a while I was the biggest star in the country. And this was at a time when other stars included Clark Gable, Jimmy Cagney, and Spencer Tracy. I was at the top. But when I did this picture with Hope I couldn't get arrested. Some of the pictures I made at this time weren't released, they escaped! But Hope knew I would be good in the role and he insisted on me. I never forgot that.

When told of Rooney's sentiments, Hope said to journalist Gary Schneeberger, "I always liked Mickey and thought he did a great job in the picture. I never realized at the time that I was helping him out so much. I just wanted him in the picture. But if I helped him the way he remembers, well I'm glad I did."

The story for *Off Limits* is fairly standard and the songs are unmemorable, but, mostly due to the talented cast, it still emerges as one of the best Hope pictures of the 1950s.

One highlight features a nauseous Hogan trying to shout instructions during a fight while a fellow soldier keeps eating in front of him, making him sicker and less effective. Another has Hogan gleefully destroying what he believes to be the gangsters' automobile, only to find that it belongs to a superior officer.

Rooney was a natural athlete, so the fight scenes are well played. Rooney had donned the gloves quite effectively for the 1947 MGM drama *Killer McCoy* and got back in shape for this film. The final match allows him to work opposite fellow child star Stanley "Stosh" Clements, who had a reputation for being particularly good in boxing scenes (notably in the film *Salty O'Rourke*). The two actors knew and respected each other and it shows in their scenes.

Rooney told this writer:

> I had known "Stosh" Clements since we were kids, so it was great to
> see each other again. He was a great actor, one of those guys who could
> play it straight or for laughs. Whatever the script had him do and what-
> ever the director wanted, Stosh would get it done.

Off Limits is a perfectly enjoyable Bob Hope comedy that is bolstered
by a strong supporting cast.

Here Come the Girls

Directed by Claude Binyon. Writing Credits: Edmund L. Hartmann and Hal Kanter. Produced by Paul Jones. Original Music by Ray Evans and Jay Livingston. Cinematography by Lionel Lindon. Film Editing by Arthur P. Schmidt. Art Direction by Roland Anderson and Hal Pereira. Set Decoration by Sam Comer and Grace Gregory. Costume Design by Edith Head. Makeup by Wally Westmore. Assistant Director: Edward Salven. Sound by John Cope and Hugo Grenzbach. Special Effects by Gordon Jennings and Paul K. Lerpae. Choreography by Nick Castle.

Cast: Bob Hope (Stanley Snodgrass); Tony Martin (Allen Trent); Arlene Dahl (Irene Bailey); Rosemary Clooney (Daisy Crockett); Millard Mitchell (Albert Snodgrass); William Demarest (Dennis Logan); Fred Clark (Harry Fraser); Robert Strauss (Jack the Slasher); Zamah Cunningham (Mrs. Snodgrass); Frank Orth (Mr. Hungerford); Johnny Downs (Bob); Phyllis Coates (Chorus Girl); Inesita (Spanish Dancer); Maceo Anderson, Loren Brown, Everett Corelli, Jimmy Hunt and Alex Jackson (bit parts); Rufus L. McDonald, Hugh Sanders, Prince C. Spencer and Alfred T. Williams (The Four Step Brothers).

Released October 22, 1953, by Paramount Pictures.

Here Come the Girls is another of Bob Hope's weaker films. Hope plays Stanley Snodgrass, an entertainer whose abilities are so meager that he gets fired from his job as a singer. When the show's new lead (Tony Martin) is stalked by a killer (Robert Strauss) who has designs on the show's leading lady (Arlene Dahl), Snodgrass is rehired to throw the killer off the track.

Using the Hope character as bait in order to entrap a killer is a method that worked well in *Monsieur Beaucaire*. With *Here Come the Girls*, however, there is a noticeable lack of enthusiasm for the material.

The musical numbers are basically dull, especially when Tony Martin is on screen (Martin has the distinction of performing the worst song in a Marx Brothers picture: "Tenement Symphony" from *The Big Store*). Perhaps the Four Step Brothers come off best in the music sequences.

Hope and Rosemary Clooney in *Here Come the Girls* (1953).

The slapstick finale is amusing, but it is hardly enough to bolster the rest of the picture. It is similar in structure to the MGM feature *Go West* (1940) in which the Marx Brothers lethargically amble about a tiresome western plot until a slapstick train sequence concludes the film on a high note. By that time, the film has already failed.

During this point in his career, Hope embarked on a weekly television series while still maintaining his film career and radio show as well as live performances. Perhaps he was spreading himself too thin, which could be the reason he appears to offer little energy or enthusiasm to this project.

During filming of *Here Come the Girls*, Hope hooked up with Crosby and did a brief cameo in the Dean Martin and Jerry Lewis picture *Scared Stiff*. Martin and Lewis were currently the hottest attraction in movies. Ironically, *Scared Stiff* was a remake of *The Ghost Breakers*.

Casanova's Big Night

Directed by Norman Z. McLeod. Writing Credits: Aubrey Wisberg, Hal Kanter and Edmund L. Hartmann. Produced by Paul Jones. Original Music by Jay Livingston and Lyn Murray. Cinematography by Lionel Lindon. Film Editing by Ellsworth Hoagland. Art Direction by Albert Nozaki and Hal Pereira. Set Decoration by Sam Comer and Ross Dowd. Costume Design by Edith Head and Yvonne Wood. Makeup Department: Wally Westmore. Assistant Director: Michael D. Moore. Sound by Gene Garvin and Gene Merritt. Special Effects by John P. Fulton and Farciot Edouart. Choreography by Josephine Earl.

Cast: Bob Hope (Pippo Popolino); Joan Fontaine (Francesca Bruni); Audrey Dalton (Elena Di Gambetta); Basil Rathbone (Lucio/Narrator); Hugh Marlowe (Stefano Di Gambetta); Arnold Moss (The Doge); John Carradine (Foressi); John Hoyt (Maggiorin); Hope Emerson (Duchess of Castelbello); Robert Hutton (Raphael, Duc of Castelbello); Vincent Price (Casanova); Lon Chaney, Jr. (Emo the Murderer); Raymond Burr (Bragadin); Frieda Inescort (Signora Di Gambetta); Primo Carnera (Corfa); Frank Puglia (Carabaccio); Paul Cavanagh (Signor Alberto Di Gambetta); Romo Vincent (Giovanni); Henry Brandon (Captain Rugello); Natalie Schafer (Signora Foressi); Douglas Fowley (Second Prisoner); Nestor Paiva (Gnocchi); Barbara Freking (Maria); Joan Shawlee (Beatrice D'brizzi); Oliver Blake (Amadeo the Cabinet Maker); Fritz Feld (Diplomat); Bess Flowers (Marquesa); Eric Alden (Maggiorin's Ruffian); Paul Newlan (Regniacci); Charles Hicks (Assistant Headsman); Richard Karlan (Outside Guard); Walter Kingsford (Minister); Lucien Littlefield (First Prisoner); Torben Meyer (Attendant); Dan Dowling (Cloth Merchant); Kathryn Grant and Marla English (Girls on Bridge); Arline Hunter (Girl in Window); Keith Richards (Servant); Michael Ross (Jailer); Dick Sands (Headsman); Rexene Stevens (Swimmer); Joe Gray (Court Guard); Skelton Knaggs (Little Man); Charles Cooley (Manservant); Gino Corrado (Ambassador); John Doucette (Mounted Guard); Joseph Vitale (Guard on Steps); John Alderson (Outside Guard); Trippe Elan (Small Boy); Anthony Warde (bit part).

Released April 17, 1954, by Paramount Pictures.

THE HILARIOUS STORY OF
HISTORY'S GREATEST WOLF!

CASANOVA'S BIG NIGHT

COLOR BY
TECHNICOLOR

Bob's hilarious
as the menace
of Venice!

starring

BOB HOPE
JOAN FONTAINE

and Co-starring

BASIL RATHBONE · AUDREY DALTON · HUGH MARLOWE

Produced by Paul Jones · Directed by Norman Z. McLeod
Written for the Screen by Hal Kanter and Edmund Hartmann
Based on a Story by Aubrey Wisberg · A Paramount Picture

Casanova's Big Night was quite an improvement over *Here Come the Girls* and remains one of the better Hope films from this period.

Hope plays Pippo Popolino, a tailor's apprentice who agrees to impersonate the great lover Casanova. A duchess (Hope Emerson) wants to test the fidelity of her son's fiancée (Joan Fontaine), so Pippo will receive a large sum of money if he succeeds in seducing her.

Fast-paced, colorful, and very funny, *Casanova's Big Night* recalls one of Hope's best films, *Monsieur Beaucaire*. Along with many funny lines by Hope, the supporting cast is filled with top attractions, such as Vincent Price, John Carradine, Lon Chaney, Jr., Raymond Burr, and Basil Rathbone.

Rathbone comes off very well as Lucio, the former servant of the actual Casanova, who is going along with Pippo's charade. At one point he states, "You'll never be anyone other than Pippo Popolino and I can't think of anything more insulting!"

During a prison sequence, Pippo asks a prisoner the time. "Oh, about 1758," is the reply. While riding in a gondola, Pippo puts his hand in the water, sniffs, and states, "Canal Number 5!" When he is about to be executed, he breaks down the actor's fourth wall and addresses the audience directly, pleading that they spare his life.

Hope takes good advantage of the many opportunities for his characteristic humor in *Casanova's Big Night*. It is briskly paced and holds up very well.

Opposite page: Ad for *Casanova's Big Night*, 1954.

The Seven Little Foys

Directed by Melville Shavelson. Writing Credits: Jack Rose and Melville Shavelson. Produced by Jack Rose. Cinematography by John F. Warren. Film Editing by Ellsworth Hoagland. Art Direction by John B. Goodman and Hal Pereira. Set Decoration by Sam Comer and Frank R. McKelvy. Costume Design by Edith Head. Makeup by Wally Westmore. Assistant Directors: Michael D. Moore and James A. Rosenberger. Sound by John Cope and Harry Lindgren. Special Effects by John P. Fulton and Farciot Edouart. Choreography by Nick Castle.

Cast: Bob Hope (Eddie Foy); Milly Vitale (Madeleine Morando Foy); George Tobias (Barney Green); Angela Clarke (Clara Morando); Herbert Heyes (Judge); Richard Shannon (Stage Manager); Billy Gray (Brynie Foy); Lee Erickson (Charley Foy); Paul De Rolf (Richard Foy); Lydia Reed (Mary Foy); Linda Bennett (Madeleine Foy); Jimmy Baird (Eddie Foy, Jr.); Tommy Duran (Irving Foy); Charley Foy (Narrator [Voice]); James Cagney (George M. Cohan); Jerry Mathers (Brynie [Age 5]); Milton Frome (Driscoll); King Donovan (Harrison); Lester Matthews (Father O'Casey); Oliver Blake (Santa Claus); Jimmy Conlin (Stage Doorman); Joe Flynn (Priest); Marian Carr (Soubrette); Noel Drayton (Priest); Lewis Martin (Minister); Joe Evans and George Boyce (Elephant Act); Dabbs Greer (Tutor); Harry Cheshire (Stage Doorman at "Iroquois"); Billy Nelson (Customs Inspector); Jack Pepper (Theatre Manager); Betty Uitti (Dance Double); Renata Vanni (Ballerina Mistress).

Released May 31, 1955, by Paramount Pictures.

As his dramatic role in *Sorrowful Jones* was artistically successful and a box office hit, Hope felt he was ready to tackle an even meatier part.

Eddie Foy was a top vaudeville star who was noted as one of the most self-centered men in show business history. Hope's eminent likeability makes it difficult to accept him in such a role, but he manages to be quite believable in recreating Foy, a man who neglected his wife and family for his career.

Foy's wife was a beautiful Italian dancer who bore him seven children. She was a devoted wife and mother, but Foy constantly cheated on her and

Hope dances with James Cagney in *The Seven Little Foys* (1955).

gave almost no attention to the children. She became seriously ill and died at a young age, leaving Foy to care for the seven children.

Hope must play the most serious scenes of his career when, as Foy, he is told the news of his wife's death. The night before he was to film this difficult scene, Hope's long-time friend Barney Dean died of cancer. As Dean lay dying, he summoned Hope closer to him. He smiled and whispered, "Any thing you want me to tell Jolson?" Entertainer Al Jolson, a mutual friend, had died a couple of years before. Shortly after that quip, Dean himself was gone.

Hope, devastated by the loss of his close friend, used this sorrow to effectively play the scene where Foy confronts his wife's death.

Foy then maintains his career by training his children and bringing them into the act as the Seven Little Foys.

Easily the highlight of this film, and one of the highlights of Hope's entire movie career, is his challenge dance with James Cagney, who appears in the part of George M. Cohan. Cagney won an Oscar for his portrayal of Cohan in the 1942 classic *Yankee Doodle Dandy* and was eager to revisit the role. He also insisted on doing the part for free. Cagney recalled that when he was a small-time vaudeville performer, he could always count on a meal at the Foy home. This was his way of paying them back.

Cagney also recalled that when he hopped up on the table to do the dance with Hope, pain shot through both of his knees. He got through the number, but afterward in the dressing room, Hope was astonished to see how Cagney's knees had swelled. When viewing the film, Cagney's pained grimace as he first jumps onto the table is indeed noticeable. Despite this, he does his usual wonderful job.

Jerry Mathers, who is best known as television's Beaver Cleaver, had a small role in this film. In an interview with this writer, he recalled, "Mr. Hope was a great guy. There were a lot of kids on the set, and he was really patient with us and a lot of fun. I worked with him again, and he was just as kind. Those films were great to do."

The Seven Little Foys was a major box office hit, and critics were impressed with Hope's dramatic performance. *The New York Daily News* stated:

> Hope doesn't have to take any more insults from Bing Crosby about his acting. Hope can now hold up his head with Hollywood's dramatic thespians as for the first time in his career, Hope isn't appearing as Hope on screen. He's acting and doing a commendable job.

Once again, Hope felt he could possibly get an Oscar nomination for his performance in a dramatic film. And once again, he wasn't nominated.

That Certain Feeling

Directed by Melvin Frank and Norman Panama. Writing Credits: William Altman, Norman Panama, Melvin Frank and I.A.L. Diamond. Based on the play "Knave of Hearts" by Jean Kerr and Eleanor Brooke. Produced by Melvin Frank and Norman Panama. Original Music by Joseph J. Lilley, Harold Arlen and James F. Hanley. Non-Original Music by George Gershwin and Ira Gershwin. Cinematography by Loyal Griggs. Film Editing by Tom McAdoo. Art Direction by Henry Bumstead and Hal Pereira. Costume Design by Edith Head. Assistant Director: Francisco Day. Choreography by Nick Castle.

Cast: Bob Hope (Francis X. Dignan); Eva Marie Saint (Dunreath Henry); George Sanders (Larry Larkin); Pearl Bailey (Gussie); David Lewis (Joe Wickes); Al Capp (himself); Jerry Mathers (Norman Taylor); Herbert Rudley (Doctor); Florenz Ames (Senator Winston); Douglas Wood (Senator); Paul Dubov and Herb Vigran (TV Directors); Jeff Hayden (TV Technician); Jeanette Miller, Jacqueline Beer and Valerie Allen (Models); Richard Shannon (Cab Driver); Jan Bradley, Lawrence Dobkin, Eric Alden, Richard Keene, Joe Kerr and Jack Lomas (bit parts).

Released July 2, 1956, by Paramount Pictures.

That Certain Feeling can be considered an interesting failure.

Hope plays Francis Dignan, a cartoonist who must "ghost" a strip for fellow artist Larry Larkin (George Sanders), who has lost his touch. Dignan's ex-wife (Eva Marie Saint) is engaged to Larkin, adding to the complications.

While the plot is thin, Eva Marie Saint is nowhere near as good a comic actress as she is a dramatic actress, and Sanders appears more bored than usual, there are some interesting things about *That Certain Feeling*.

Hope is essentially appearing as a much older version of the iconoclast that can be found in a film like *Road to Singapore*. Dignan is an artist who is devoted to his craft and has a free-thinking attitude and dedication to what he believes in. The stuffy Larkin is the conservative opposition whose own

121

Ad for *That Certain Feeling*, 1956.

abilities have dissipated. It provides for an interesting, ironic subtext, but the film is rather dull.

Jerry Mathers recalled that Hope cast some of his own children as Mathers's playmates so that the young actor would have someone to keep him company on the set filled with adults. In an interview with the author, Mathers still fondly remembered Hope's kindness toward him.

Pearl Bailey comes off best in this forgettable film, rising above her role as a domestic.

Despite *That Certain Feeling* being one of Hope's less interesting films, it has been well received in some circles. There are Hope biographies that cite *That Certain Feeling* as a solid example of Hope using humor within the character rather than relying on the steady stream of prepared jokes as had been his forte. At least one movie source book, Steven Scheuer's *Movies on TV*, considers *That Certain Feeling* among Hope's better films of this period.

While the film does have some interest, its overall success is limited to this surface interest. It isn't among the best work of any of its actors.

The Iron Petticoat

Directed by Ralph Thomas. Writing Credits: Ben Hecht and Harry Saltz-
man. Produced by Betty E. Box and Harry Saltzman. Original Music by
Benjamin Frankel. Cinematography by Ernest Steward. Film Editing by
Frederick Wilson. Art Direction by Carmen Dillon. Makeup by W. T.
Partleton. Production Management: Denis Holt. Assistant Director: James
H. Ware. Art Department: Vernon Dixon. Sound by Roger Cherrill, Gor-
don K. McCallum and John W. Mitchell.

Cast: Bob Hope (Major Chuck Lockwood); Katharine Hepburn (Vinka
Kovelenko); Noelle Middleton (Connie); James Robertson Justice (Col-
onel Sklarnoff); Robert Helpmann (Ivan Kropotkin); David Kossoff (Dr.
Dubratz); Alan Gifford (Colonel Tarbell); Nicholas Phipps (Tony Mal-
lard); Paul Carpenter (Major Lewis); Sid James (Paul); Alexander Gauge
(Senator Holly); Sandra Dorne (Tityana); Richard Wattis (Lingerie Clerk);
Tutte Lemkow (Sutsiyawa); Martin Boddey (Grisha); Maria Antippas
(Sklarnoff's Secretary); Man Mountain Dean (Russian Strongarm Man);
Doris Goddard (Maria).

Released January 7, 1957, by Metro Goldwyn Mayer.

One of the least-seen Hope films, and deservedly so, *The Iron Petticoat*
is a botched attempt at reworking *Ninotchka*.

Bob Hope plays Chuck Norwood, an English captain eager to marry
into the British upper class; Kate Hepburn plays Vinka Kovelenko, a tough-
as-nails Russian flying ace who defects because she feels discriminated against
in Communist Russia.

The film was plagued with problems from the outset.

Cary Grant was originally slated to play the lead role opposite Hepburn but had to bow out due to another commitment. Hope was asked to
fill in and was flattered at the opportunity to work opposite Katharine Hepburn.

Hope wanted the film revamped for his talents, hiring several of his own
writers to fill the dialog with jokes and asides. Screenwriter Ben Hecht crafted

Ad for *The Iron Petticoat*, 1957.

a different screenplay from what Hope was used to, and while Hope had proven himself as a dramatic actor, he didn't want to do a comedy that was outside of his established style. Hope felt, and with some validity, that his fans would expect a more joke-filled script than Hecht had prepared.

Hecht walked out on the project, and Hope had his retinue of writers provide a series of jokes to liven up the movie.

The film was a disaster artistically and commercially and remains one of Hope's worst films.

Upon its release, Ben Hecht took out a full-page ad in the *Hollywood Reporter*:

> My dear partner Bob Hope,
>
> This is to notify you that I have removed my name as author from our mutilated venture *The Iron Petticoat*. Unfortunately, your other partner, Katharine Hepburn, can't shy out of the fractured picture with me. Although her magnificent comic performance has been blow-torched out of the film, there is enough left of the Hepburn footage to identify her for the sharpshooters. I am assured by my hopeful predators that *The Iron Petticoat* will go over big with people "who can't get enough of Bob Hope." Let us hope this swooning contingent is not confined to yourself and your euphoric agent, Louis Shurr.

Beau James

Directed by Melville Shavelson. Written by Jack Rose and Melville Shavelson. From the novel by Gene Fowler. Produced by Jack Rose. Original Music by Richard Rodgers, Lorenz Hart and James J. "Jimmy" Walker. Cinematography by John F. Warren. Film Editing by Floyd Knudtson. Art Direction by John B. Goodman and Hal Pereira. Set Decoration by Sam Comer and Frank R. McKelvy. Costume Design by Edith Head. Makeup by Wally Westmore. Sound Department: Charles Grenzbach and Hugo Grenzbach. Special Effects by John P. Fulton. Choreography by Jack Baker. Singing Voice for Vera Miles: Imogene Lynn.

Cast: Bob Hope (Mayor James J. "Jimmy" Walker); Vera Miles (Betty Compton); Paul Douglas (Chris Nolan); Alexis Smith (Allie Walker); Sid Melton (Sid Nash); Darren McGavin (Charley Hand); Walter Winchell (Narrator); Joe Mantell (Bernie Williams); Horace McMahon (Prosecutor); Richard Shannon (Dick Jackson); Willis Bouchey (Arthur Julian); Walter Catlett (Al Smith); Jack Benny (Guest); Jack Pepper (Gangster); Jimmy Durante and George Jessel (themselves).

Released June 7, 1957, by Paramount Pictures.

After having done essentially a dramatic interpretation of his usual screen character in *Sorrowful Jones* and nailing a solid dramatic role in *The Seven Little Foys*, Hope apparently felt he was ready to stretch further.

While Eddie Foy was in show business, allowing Hope to understand the nuances of character, Jimmy Walker was a New York political figure of the Roaring Twenties. It was quite unlike any character Hope had played in his career, and he rises to the occasion with the sort of commitment that can only net a job well done.

Walker, the mayor of New York, was not the sort of staid political figure that would come across as merely dull on screen. He was given to singing, dancing, wisecracking, and cavorting, not terribly unlike Hope's usual screen persona. The depth of Walker's character is mined rather well, however, with Hope giving his all in every scene.

The story deals with Walker's initial forays into politics, being thrust into the position of mayor of Gotham. He doesn't take the job seriously and is passive about the surrounding corruption. As his political career rises and his own corruption is evident, the film spends perhaps a bit too much time on Walker's affair with actress Betty Compton (Vera Miles).

Director Melville Shavelson, who co-wrote the screenplay based on Gene Fowler's biography, does a nice job of capturing the spirit of the 1920s, while appearances by George Jessel and Jimmy Durante add flavor.

The supporting cast is strong. Along with Miles, Alexis Smith, while cast against type, does a good job as Walker's long-suffering wife Alice. Paul Douglas is excellent as the powerful force of Tammany, who helps boost Walker's political career.

Hope's film career received a boost of its own with this film. While he no longer was among the top box office stars in America, his radio show had ended, and he stopped doing a regular television series, Hope still had the sort of command to generate good box office, even in an offbeat role. After this film, many had greater respect for his acting prowess. Unfortunately, his cinematic output remained sporadic and soon spiraled downhill rather quickly. Despite his very good work as Jimmy Walker, Hope's best movies were already behind him.

Paris Holiday

Directed by Gerd Oswald. Written by Bob Hope, Edmund Beloin and Dean Riesner. Produced by Bob Hope and C. R. Foster-Kemp. Original Music by Joseph J. Lilley, Jimmy Van Heusen and Sammy Cahn. Cinematography by Roger Hubert. Film Editing by Ellsworth Hoagland. Production Design by Georges Wakhévitch. Costume Design by Pierre Balmain. Makeup by Hagop Arakelian and Boris Karabanoff. Assistant Director: Paul Feyder. Sound by Robert Biard and Francis J. Scheid.

Cast: Bob Hope (Robert Leslie Hunter); Fernandel (Fernydel); Anita Ekberg (Zara); Martha Hyer (Ann McCall); Preston Sturges (Serge Vitry); Maurice Teynac (Doctor Bernais); Yves Brainville (Inspector Dupont); Jean Murat (Judge); André Morell (American Ambassador); Alan Gifford (American Consul); Hans Verner (Gangster); Paul Violette and Marcel Pérès (Institute Guards); Roger Tréville (Patient); Irène Tunc (Shipboard Lovely).

Released May 9, 1958, by United Artists.

Another of Hope's least interesting films, *Paris Holiday* seems to have great possibilities.

Hope provided the original story, contributed to the screenplay, and acted as the film's producer. French comedian Fernandel is cleverly cast to play opposite Hope. The film is made in the same fashion as his most successful comedy mysteries, *My Favorite Blonde* and *My Favorite Brunette*.

And still the movie falls flat.

Hope is Bob Hunter, an American comedian on a liner to France. He is interested in securing the rights to a new play. His friend and counterpart is Fernydel (Fernandel), a French comedian who is working with him.

Hunter is being trailed by the mysterious Zara (Anita Ekberg), while at the same time he is pursuing Ann McCall (Martha Hyer), a diplomat. Zara is after the French manuscript, which she believes is in Hunter's possession, but Hunter is unaware why. The pursuit continues through Paris.

Highlights include a scene set in an amusement park, Hunter being rescued by helicopter from a mental hospital, and a mildly funny courtroom

Ad for *Paris Holiday*, 1958.

sequence in which the Gallic Fernydel attempts to speak for Hunter's sanity despite his limited English skills. In an effort to appear hip, Fernydel uses all of the popular catch phrases Hunter has taught him ("crazy," "out of this world," etc.). Although slightly amusing, this scene pales in comparison to a similar sequence with the Wiere Brothers in *Road to Rio* (1947).

It is fairly interesting to see writer-director Preston Sturges (*Hail the Conquering Hero*, *Sullivan's Travels*, *Miracle of Morgan's Creek*) in one of his few acting roles, and this is Fernandel's only appearance in an American movie. Other than those novelties, however, *Paris Holiday* is a throwaway.

Paris Holiday went millions over budget and was as much a financial disappointment as it was an artistic one.

Alias Jesse James

Directed by Norman Z. McLeod. Writing Credits: Daniel B. Beauchamps, William Bowers, Bert Lawrence and Robert St. Aubrey. Produced by Bob Hope, Jack Hope and Kent McCray. Original Music by Arthur Altman, By Bunham, Bud Burtson, Joseph Hooven and Marilyn Hooven. Cinematography by Lionel Lindon. Film Editing by Jack Bachom and Marvin Coil. Production Design by Roland Anderson and Hal Pereira. Set Decoration by Sam Comer and Bertram C. Granger. Costume Design by Edith Head. Makeup by Wally Westmore, Nellie Manley and Bill Morley. Assistant Directors: Daniel McCauley and William Watson. Sound by Lyle Figland and Charles Grenzbach. Special Effects by John P. Fulton and Farciot Edouart.

Cast: Bob Hope (Milford Farnsworth); Rhonda Fleming (Cora Lee Collins); Wendell Corey (T. J. "Jesse" James); Gloria Talbott (Princess Irawanie); Jim Davis (Frank James); Will Wright (Titus Queasley); Mary Young ("Ma" James); Bob Gunderson, Fred Kohler, Jr., Ethan Laidlaw and Glenn Strange (James Gang); Richard Alexander (Jeremiah Cole, Blacksmith); Ward Bond (Major Seth Adams); Nestor Paiva (Grigsby, Miner with Goat); Michael Ross (Grigsby's Killer); Oliver Blake (Mortimer Hopelaw, Undertaker); Scatman Crothers (Railroad Porter); I. Stanford Jolley (2nd Conductor); Jack Lambert (Snake Brice); Lyle Latell (First Train Conductor); Wally Brown (Bartender, Dirty Dog Saloon); Mike Mazurki (Tough in Dirty Dog Saloon); Mickey Finn (2nd Tough in Dirty Dog Saloon); J. Anthony Hughes (Dirty Dog Saloonkeeper); James Burke (Charlie, NYC Bartender); Sid Melton (Fight Fan); Emory Parnell (Angel's Rest Sheriff); George E. Stone (Gibson Girl Fan [NYC Bar]); Harry Tyler (Elmo, the Station Master); Joseph Vitale (Sam Hiawatha); Gary Cooper, Roy Rogers and Gene Autry (themselves); Fess Parker (Davy Crockett); Jay Silverheels (Tonto); Hugh O'Brian (Wyatt Earp); James Garner (Bret Maverick); Gail Davis (Annie Oakley); James Arness (Marshal Matt Dillon); Bing Crosby (himself).

Released March 20, 1959, by United Artists.

Ad for *Alias Jesse James*, 1959.

Alias Jesse James stands out as one of Hope's funniest films and is easily his best all-out comedy feature since *Son of Paleface*.

Hope plays Milford Farnsworth, a big-city insurance salesman who unwittingly sells a life insurance policy to Jesse James (Wendell Corey) at a bar. When his employer (Will Wright) finds out that Jesse James is a policy holder in the company, he becomes incensed, realizing the gunfighter is a very poor insurance risk. Farnsworth is sent to the West to protect Jesse from harm.

While out West, Farnsworth falls for Jesse James's girl, Cora Lee Collins (Rhonda Fleming).

Perhaps the failure of *Paris Holiday* prompted Hope, who is the film's executive producer, to revisit the type of comedy that was his biggest success. There are echoes of his classic *Paleface* films throughout *Alias Jesse James*.

The film's greatest sequence is the shootout at the end, during which Hope expertly does a send-up of *The Paleface*. In the original, Hope, as Painless Potter, believed he was killing Indians when in fact it was Calamity Jane (Jane Russell) doing the shooting from a hidden area. In *Alias Jesse James*, Farnsworth is shooting at the bandits and hitting nothing, but once again he is helped by a more effective shooter. Only this time the assistance comes from movie and television cowboy stars Roy Rogers, Gene Autry, Gary Cooper, James Garner (as Bret Maverick), Gail Davis (as Annie Oakley), Hugh O'Brien (as Wyatt Earp), Jay Silverheels (as Tonto), and Fess Parker (as Davy Crockett).

One can't overestimate the popularity of western films in movies and on television during the late 1950s. The power of these stars was enormous and would have greatly increased box office potential. Hope wisely thought from an artistic perspective, however, and did not tip off these cameos in any of the advertising for *Alias Jesse James*. As a result, the appearances were a huge surprise and were loudly cheered, especially by younger moviegoers.

Hope seemed to realize he was working in a better, funnier movie than he'd been churning out as of late. His performance has the sort of comedic enthusiasm absent since perhaps *Casanova's Big Night*. While this sort of passion is evident in his dramatic forays *The Seven Little Foys* and *Beau James*, there wasn't much comedy to get enthused about in failures like *Here Come the Girls, That Certain Feeling, The Iron Petticoat,* and *Paris Holiday.*

Alias Jesse James, however, did not signal another stretch of solid comedy films from Hope. It was, in fact, the last good Bob Hope comedy save for the offbeat *The Facts of Life* that followed.

The Facts of Life

Directed by Melvin Frank. Writing Credits: Melvin Frank and Norman Panama. Produced by Hal C. Kern and Norman Panama. Original Music by Leigh Harline and Johnny Mercer. Cinematography by Charles Lang. Film Editing by Frank Bracht. Production Design by J. McMillan Johnson and Kenneth A. Reid. Costume Design by Edith Head and Edward Stevenson. Assistant Director: Jack Aldworth.

Cast: Bob Hope (Larry Gilbert); Lucille Ball (Kitty Weaver); Ruth Hussey (Mary Gilbert); Don DeFore (Jack Weaver); Louis Nye (Hamilton "Ham" Busbee); Philip Ober (Doc Mason); Marianne Stewart (Connie Mason); Peter Leeds (Thompson); Hollis Irving (Myrtle Busbee); Addison Richards (Larry's Boss); Louise Beavers (Gussie, Gilberts' Maid [as Louise Beaver]); Mike Mazurki (Husband in Hotel Room); Vito Scotti (Fishing Boat Driver); Bernard Fein (Man in Motel Room); Bess Flowers (Woman at Airport); William Lanteau (Airline Clerk); Robert F. Simon (Hotel Clerk); John Indrisano (Bartender); Joe Ploski (Man at Drive-In); Bert Stevens (Man at Airport); Jeffrey Sayre (Nightclub Dance Extra).

Released November 16, 1960, by United Artists.

The Facts of Life is a more sophisticated, mature comedy for both Hope and Lucille Ball, and their performances are among the best of their respective careers.

Hope is Larry Gilbert, a middle-aged businessman who has become a bit settled in his humdrum life. He has a good job, a good family, and all seems right with his world. However, he is entering a midlife crisis. He has become bored and doesn't quite know what he wants to change. Even his occasional getaways have become less interesting.

Lucy is Kitty Weaver, an equally bored housewife whose husband works with Gilbert. Kitty finds Gilbert to be rather boorish, while he dismisses her as a petty annoyance.

The Gilberts and the Weavers plan a vacation together. Both Larry's wife and Kitty's husband become ill, so Larry and Kitty are stuck doing things together. They very gradually develop a mutual respect, then a friendship, and, eventually, fall in love.

It is important to note how well written this Panama-Frank script is and how well Bob Hope and Lucille Ball play the roles. This is not Hope's quips and Lucy's wild slapstick antics. Each performer truly embodies his or her character, really bringing to life the mutual boredom of a limited lifestyle and the gradual taboo relationship. While Hope has always been good with dialog, especially jokes, his facial expressions as Larry very slowly warms up to Kitty are as telling as anything provided by the screenwriters. He conveys interest as well as guilt. Lucy's display of confused apprehension is equally effective.

Hope is often chided for continuing to play the youthful girl-chaser well into his fifties. To some extent, this is justified, but in *The Facts of Life* he seems quite comfortable in an age-appropriate role that dares to show how infidelity can occur with people who feel stifled by their very existence. It challenges what the culture had been presenting as the quintessential lifestyle.

As the film progresses, Kitty and Larry fall in love and plan to leave their respective spouses. However, the free paradise they had enjoyed when thrust together doesn't occur when they go off for a secret rendezvous. They run into mutual friends, their car breaks down in a rainstorm, they must battle the elements in a rustic cabin, and their verbal exchanges are sharper and eventually evolve into an argument. They begin to see things through more realistic eyes, obliterating the starry eyed romanticism on which they'd foolishly tried to build their relationship.

Kitty brings up the fact that she would be maintaining custody of her children, while Larry would likely lose custody of his. The idea of their respective spouses remarrying is also discussed. Eventually, they realize their relationship is best left as a brief encounter that is never again discussed.

Hope was initially apprehensive about doing the film, figuring it wasn't funny enough. Ms. Ball, however, liked the script and was surprised that such a mature screenplay was written by the men who had also penned some of the most comical Road pictures.

The Facts of Life was a real departure for all involved, was a box office hit and critical success, and has held up well.

Bachelor in Paradise

Directed by Jack Arnold. Screenplay by Hal Kanter. Story by Vera Caspary and Valentine Davies. Produced by Ted Richmond. Original Music by Henry Mancini. Cinematography by Joseph Ruttenberg. Film Editing by Richard W. Farrell. Art Direction by George W. Davis and Hans Peters. Set Decoration by F. Keogh Gleason and Henry Grace. Costume Design by Helen Rose. Makeup by William Tuttle. Assistant Director: Erich von Stroheim, Jr. Sound by Franklin Milton.

Cast: Bob Hope (Adam J. Niles); Lana Turner (Rosemary Howard); Janis Paige (Dolores Jynson); Jim Hutton (Larry Delavane); Paula Prentiss (Linda Delavane); Roberta Shore (Ginnie); Don Porter (Thomas W. Jynson); Virginia Grey (Camille Quinlaw); Agnes Moorehead (Judge Peterson); Florence Sundstrom (Mrs. Pickering); John McGiver (Austin Palfrey); Clinton Sundberg (Rodney Jones); Alan Hewitt (Attorney Backett); Reta Shaw (Mrs. Brown); Bill Zucker (W. P. Mathews, Assistant Commissioner); Roy Engel (McCracken); Mauritz Hugo (Rodwell); Royce Kane (Mrs. Carding); John Lawrence (Mike Carding); Sean Peters (Peter); Eddie Rosson (Steve Delavane); Dick Whittinghill (Bruce Freedman); Tracy Stratford (Mrs. McGonigle); Mary Treen (Housewife); Robert Williams (Fireman); Olan Soule (Waiter); Jerry Doggett and Vin Scully (themselves, Dodgers Game Announcers).

Released November 1, 1961, by Metro Goldwyn Mayer.

Bachelor in Paradise is an interesting hybrid. It is partly a more mature, sophisticated comedy as was *The Facts of Life*; however it also contains elements of the more traditional Bob Hope pictures. The blend works reasonably well. This is far from Hope's best work, but it is not bad for this period of his career.

Hope plays Adam J. Niles, a romance writer whose work is popular with ladies. Because of his success in this field, he is something of a ladies' man. His bachelor status makes him even more attractive to married women who feel suppressed by their current status, and his way with words makes him appear more caring and a better listener than any average husband. When he moves into a suburban neighborhood in order to research lifestyles for his next writing project, he is beset by interested housewives and annoyed breadwinners.

As with *The Facts of Life*, Hope plays someone who is middle aged rather than the youthful skirt-chaser of yore. However, this time he finds himself the center of attention amid a bevy of attractive women who feel trapped by their own domesticity, just as he and Lucille Ball had been in *The Facts of Life*.

However, *Bachelor in Paradise* offers us a much different character for Hope. He is, instead, a very droll, very wry writer whose literary contributions are shallow but successful and allow him a certain artistic aura that attracts the average housewife who yearns for excitement and change.

That said, Lana Turner is rather miscast as the only single woman in Adam's immediate world. Her movie star looks do not illustrate her character as a small town girl. Jim Hutton (father of actor Timothy Hutton) and Paula Prentiss are well cast as the typical couple from this period, exhibiting the sort of conservative lifestyle that is threatened by the writer's arrival.

Bachelor in Paradise is a very colorful film and has held up nicely. By this time, Hope's appeal was generally to more mature audiences who had grown up watching him in his older classics like *Road to Morocco* and *The Paleface*. Kids generally relegated him to Hollywood's old guard, instead embracing the comedy of Jerry Lewis or lighter fare with Elvis Presley or Frankie Avalon. Hence, this more adult theme was successful.

Henry Mancini's musical score enhances the action nicely, while the title song was nominated for an Oscar.

The Road to Hong Kong

Directed by Norman Panama. Writing Credits: Melvin Frank and Norman Panama. Produced by Melvin Frank. Original Music by Robert Farnon, Jimmy Van Heusen and Sammy Cahn. Cinematography by Jack Hildyard. Film Editing by Alan Osbiston and John C. Smith. Production Design by Roger K. Furse. Art Direction by Syd Cain and William Hutchinson. Set Decoration by Maurice Fowler. Makeup by David Aylott. Assistant Director: Bluey Hill. Sound: A. G. Ambler, Chris Greenham and Red Law. Special Effects by Jimmy Harris, Garth Inns, Curly Nelhams, Ted Samuels and Wally Veevers. Choreographer: Jack Baker. Animators: Bob Godfrey and Keith Learner.

Cast: Bing Crosby (Harry Turner); Bob Hope (Chester Babcock); Joan Collins (Diane, 3rd Echelon Agent); Robert Morley (The Leader of the 3rd Echelon); Walter Gotell (Dr. Zorbb, 3rd Echelon Scientist); Felix Aylmer (Grand Lama); Alan Gifford (American Official); Michel Mok (Mister Ahso); Peter Sellers (Indian Neurologist Roger Delgado Jhinnah); Robert Ayres (American Official); Mei Ling (Ming Toy); Yvonne Shima (Poon Soon); Irving Allan and Harry Baird (Nubian at Lamasary); Jerry Colonna (Man Looking for a Match); Robin Hughes (American Official); Guy Standeven (Photographer at Calcutta Airport); Simon Levy (Servant); Peter Madden (Lama [Slim]): Jacqueline Jones (Blonde at Airport); John McCarthy (Messenger); Bill Nagy (Agent); Katya Douglas (3rd Echelon Receptionist); Julian Sherrier (Doctor); Dorothy Lamour (Herself); David Niven (Lama, Remembering Lady Chatterley's Lover); Frank Sinatra (The "Twig" on Plutomium); Dean Martin (The "Grape" on Plutomium); Dave King (Cameo Appearance); Zsa Zsa Gabor (Cameo Appearance [scenes deleted]).

Released May 22, 1962, by United Artists.

Perhaps the best way to indicate just how far Bob Hope had fallen is *The Road to Hong Kong,* which tries in vain to recapture the classic series entries of the past.

Opposite page: **Ad for *The Road to Hong Kong,* 1962.**

it's the most 影年最 picture you ever saw!

MELNOR FILMS LTD. PRESENTS

BING CROSBY
BOB HOPE
JOAN COLLINS

PANAMA & FRANK'S

THE ROAD TO HONG KONG

CO-STARRING OUR SPECIAL CUP OF TEA

DOROTHY LAMOUR   ROBERT MORLEY

ORIGINAL SCREENPLAY BY
NORMAN PANAMA & MELVIN FRANK

DIRECTED BY
NORMAN PANAMA

PRODUCED BY
MELVIN FRANK

A PANAMA & FRANK PRODUCTION   RELEASED THRU UNITED ARTISTS

SONGS BY SAMMY CAHN AND JIMMY VAN HEUSEN

Bing Crosby and Hope in *The Road to Hong Kong* (1962).

It probably seemed like a good idea to pair Bing and Bob for another Road picture twenty-two years after the first one and ten years after the most recent. When compared to the fun and vitality of any other *Road* picture, even the lesser entries like *Road to Bali*, this tardy effort barely registers.

Bing and Bob play Chester and Harry, con-men trying to score some fast cash in Asia. When an accident causes Chester to lose his memory, a doctor advises him of an ancient herb that will enhance his memory so greatly that it will not only return what he lost but also will allow him to memorize anything he reads.

Some confusion at an airport puts Chester in possession of the formula for rocket fuel that is to be used by our country's enemies. The duo ends up in space, battling the forces of evil.

While Bing and Bob still offer amusing banter, they sleepwalk through the picture with bored indifference. Crosby's wonderfully relaxed style and Hope's confidence delivering jokes are obliterated by two actors who don't appear to care. While poking fun at the cinematic trappings and breaking down the fourth wall were staples of the Road pictures, this later entry is simply a mild comedy with highlights that would have been mere filler in any of the earlier *Road* pictures.

There was some minor controversy early on when it was announced that Dorothy Lamour would not appear in *The Road to Hong Kong*. Long-time fans were chagrined that Bing and Bob felt she was now too old to play the ingenue (true, perhaps, but she was somewhat younger than Crosby or Hope). She was replaced by Joan Collins. After some badgering, including complaints in several newspaper columns, Dorothy was hired to do a cameo.

When they meet up with Dorothy, they tell her the story up to that point. "I better save you guys," she says, "but from the critics!"

Cameos by the likes of Dean Martin and Frank Sinatra are pleasant and amusing, but overall *The Road to Hong Kong* is a very disappointing culmination to such an engaging series of films.

Critic's Choice

Directed by Don Weis. Written by Jack Sher. From the play by Ira Levin. Produced by Frank P. Rosenberg. Original Music by George Duning. Cinematography by Charles Lang. Film Editing by William H. Ziegler. Art Direction by Edward Carrere. Set Decoration by William L. Kuehl. Costume Design by Edith Head. Makeup by Gordon Bau. Assistant Director: Russell Llewellyn. Sound Department: Stanley Jones.

Cast: Bob Hope (Parker Ballantine); Lucille Ball (Angela Ballantine); Marilyn Maxwell (Ivy London); Rip Torn (Dion Kapakos); Jessie Royce Landis (Charlotte Orr); John Dehner (S. P. Champlain); Jim Backus (Dr. William Von Hagedorn); Ricky Kelman (John Ballantine); Dorothy Green (Mrs. Champlain); Marie Windsor (Sally Orr); Joseph Gallison (Phil Yardley); Joan Shawlee (Marge Orr); Richard Deacon (Harvey Rittenhouse); Jerome Cowan (Joe Rosenfield); Donald Losby (Godfrey Von Hagedorn); Lurene Tuttle (Mother in "Sisters Three"); Ernestine Wade (Thelma); Patricia Olson (Barbara Yardley); Joy Monroe (Vicki Grant); Stanley Adams (Bartender); Theona Bryant (Beauty Operator); Art Passarella and Art Stewart (Umpires); Sam Flint and Louis Cavalier (Little League Rooters); Thomas E. Jackson (Joe, the Stage Doorman); Allan Ray (Hotel Doorman); Soupy Sales (Desk Clerk); Mimi Dillard (Maid); Hal Smith (Drunk); Stephen Coit (Waiter at Sardi's); Michael St. Angel and Ray Montgomery (Actors in "Week End"); Jimmy Gaines (Copy Boy); Frank London (The Butcher); Mike Lally and Bess Flowers (Audience Members at "Sisters Three"); Stuart Holmes (Bald Audience Member at "Sisters Three"); Desiree Sumarra (Trophy Girl); Stacy King (Telephone Operator); Ron Stokes (Party Goer); Linda Rand and Marilee Jones (Usherettes); Brenda Howard (Girlfriend); Beverly Powers and Nancy Vaughn (Girls with Dion); Rhoda Williams (Telephone Operator); Lillian Culver (Fat Woman); Elizabeth Thompson, Anita Samuels and Kelly Benson (Audience Members).

Released April 13, 1963, by Warner Brothers.

It was a good idea to once again pair Bob Hope and Lucille Ball in another mature, sophisticated comedy such as the wildly successful *The Facts of Life*.

Hope starred with Lucille Ball in *Critic's Choice* (1963).

However, this film version of Ira Levin's play about a theater critic whose wife becomes a playwright is one of Hope's worst movies.

The critic is harsh, but he is also one of the top reviewers in his field, so his words mean a great deal to the success of a production. When his wife manages to get her own play produced, he has to be honest that he doesn't like it. This leads to a variety of complications, including marital problems, threats of infidelity, and other predictable situations.

The real problem with *Critic's Choice* is that it isn't funny, Rather than being breezily paced, it is protracted and dull.

Lucille Ball, despite being typecast as the delightfully ditzy redhead of television, was quite a good actress. Of course anyone who can sustain the ditzy character she played on TV would have to be, as comedy is far more difficult to play than drama. Lucy was a trained professional and a movie veteran long before *I Love Lucy* hit the airwaves.

Bob Hope is one of comedy's greatest monologists, and his ability to offer the proper timing and inflection while delivering dialog had been firmly established by this point. He understands how to play a character connected to show business, can handle strong dramatic sequences, and is able to effortlessly shift from jokes to serious dialog without loss of aplomb.

However, in *Critics Choice*, none of this was on display. In fact a film such as this is a good example of why the baby-boomer generation did not appreciate Bob Hope until they reached adulthood and saw the older films on television. While they were growing up, Hope's film career was represented by his least interesting movies. *Critic's Choice* is an excellent example.

Bob Hope remained successful on television with variety specials and was still among the most beloved entertainers in show business. As the war in Vietnam escalated, he once again braved enemy territory to entertain the troops.

Unfortunately, his film career remained in a slump.

Call Me Bwana

Directed by Gordon Douglas. Writing Credits: Johanna Harwood and Nate Monaster. Produced by Albert R. Broccoli. Executive Producer: Harry Saltzman. Original Music by Muir Mathieson and Monty Norman. Cinematography by Ted Moore. Film Editing by Peter R. Hunt. Art Direction by Syd Cain. Set Designer: Peter Russell. Sound by Bill Daniels and John W. Mitchell. Special Effects by John Stears.

Cast: Bob Hope (Matthew Merriweather); Anita Ekberg (Luba); Edie Adams (Frederica Larson); Lionel Jeffries (Dr. Ezra Mungo); Arnold Palmer (himself); Percy Herbert (First Henchman); Paul Carpenter (Col. Spencer); Bari Jonson (Uta); Orlando Martins (Chief); Al Mulock (Second Henchman); Peter Dyneley (Williams); Mai Ling (Hyacinth); Mark Heath (Koba); Robert Nichols (American Major); Neville Monroe, Mike Moyer and Richard Burrell (Reporters); Robert Arden (1st CIA Man); Kevin Scott (2nd CIA Man).

Released June 14, 1963, by United Artists.

In another of his weakest films, Hope plays Matthew Merriweather, a writer who is a noted authority on Africa. When a returning moon capsule containing vital information goes off course and lands on the dark continent, it is discovered by a native tribe. Washington summons Merriwether to find it, not realizing that his writings are not based on experience. Meanwhile, foreign agents (Anita Ekberg, Lionel Jeffries) are sent to obtain the information and do away with Merriweather. However, the native tribe believes the capsule is holy and refuses to give it up.

Once again there are several elements here that should work. Hope is appearing as a fraud, someone whose exploits are limited to the printed page. When he must back up his literary claims, he cannot refuse and cause his lucrative writing career to be ruined. This puts him in an unusual and dangerous situation. Twenty years earlier, it likely would have worked.

The problem with *Call Me Bwana* is that nothing really goes on. The story limps along, Hope has few jokes, and it comes to a predictable conclusion.

The highlight of the entire picture is a comical golfing match between Merriweather and Arnold Palmer. However, this scene is carelessly dropped into the middle of the movie and has no connection to the story. It almost appears to have been spliced in from one of Hope's TV specials. And while amusing, it is hardly enough to make *Call Me Bwana* worthwhile.

Director Gordon Douglas is no stranger to comedy, having gotten his start at the Hal Roach studios directing Our Gang (including their Oscar winning short *Bored of Education*) and Laurel and Hardy (their 1940 feature *Saps at Sea*). Of course in the case of Laurel and Hardy, it is common knowledge that Laurel himself directed, without credit, the comedy sequences while the credited director acted as a veritable traffic cop, keeping things moving along and on schedule.

Although Douglas did direct some good films, including *Come Fill the Cup*, *Them*, and *In Like Flint*, most of his career was spent helming movies that were undistinguished (*Gildersleeve's Ghost*, *Zombies on Broadway*, *Dick Tracy Meets Cueball*) or bad (*Way, Way Out*, *Skullduggery*). *Call Me Bwana* can be classified in either category.

As with most of Hope's films during this period, critics were not impressed. A. H. Weiler of *The New York Times* stated:

> Bob Hope, one of the world's most celebrated traveling men, undoubtedly took the wrong turn when he hit the trail toward Africa for *Call Me Bwana*. Mr. Hope has been called many things in films, but tired must be the word for him, his writers, and his cast in this pseudo safari.

A Global Affair

Directed by Jack Arnold. Screenplay by Bob Fisher, Charles Lederer and Arthur Marx. Story by Eugene Vale. Produced by Hall Bartlett. Original Music by Dominic Frontiere. Cinematography by Joseph Ruttenberg. Film Editing by Bud Molin. Art Direction by E. Preston Ames and George W. Davis. Set Decoration by Henry Grace and Charles S. Thompson. Costume Design by Bill Thomas. Makeup Department: Layne Britton and William Tuttle.

Cast: Bob Hope (Frank Larrimore); Michèle Mercier (Lisette); Elga Andersen (Yvette); Yvonne De Carlo (Dolores); Miiko Taka (Fumiko); Robert Sterling (Randy Sterling); Nehemiah Persoff (Under Secretary Segura); John McGiver (Mr. Snifter); Jacques Bergerac (Guy Duval); Mickey Shaughnessy (Police Officer Dugan); Liselotte Pulver (Sonya [as Lilo Pulver]); Rafer Johnson (Nigerian Representative); Georgia Hayes (Jean); Henry Kulky (Charlie); Reta Shaw (Nurse Argyle); Hugh Downs (TV Newscaster); Billy Halop (Cab Driver); Edmon Ryan (Gavin); Tanya Lemani (Panja); Richard H. Cutting (Welland, UN Chief of Security); Voltaire Perkins (Judge in Geneva); Francis De Sales (U.S. Delegate); Booth Colman (U.N. Delegate); Rodolfo Hoyos, Jr. (Spanish Delegate); Lester Matthews (British Delegate); William Newell (Waiter); Adlai Stevenson (Cameo); Susan Hart (bit part); Martin Blaine, Ines Pedroza and François Ruggieri (People); Barbara Bouchet (Girl).

Released January 30, 1964, by United Artists.

A Global Affair is an interesting Bob Hope film to assess. It is, overall, a weak film, but because it is so much better than the last few films Hope had done, it comes off at least as good as *Bachelor in Paradise*. In any case, it is markedly superior to both *Critic's Choice* and *Call Me Bwana*.

Hope plays Frank Larrimore, an American diplomat who works in an office at the United Nations. When a baby girl is abandoned in the building, he is instructed to care for the child until her mother can be found.

Frank is a bachelor, so various attractive foreign women working at the

UN are attracted to his helplessness. They vie for a chance to help care for the child and to get Frank's attention as well.

Of course Frank becomes attached to the baby, but his single status precludes him from adopting her unless he can prove to the Security Council that he would make a good parent.

There are some amusing moments in *A Global Affair*, and although Hope was sixty-one years old, it is still fun to see him having to ward off a bevy of foreign beauties all attempting to mother the child.

One comic highlight features the United Nations delegates all catching the chicken pox from the baby, but the low point is Frank's speech to the Security Council in his effort to keep the baby. A long-winded speech about brotherhood makes for a pretty dull wrap-up.

Bosley Crowther of *The New York Times* was pleased with *A Global Affair*:

> It's a pip of an idea to have Bob Hope at the United Nations, where he probably belongs, come to think of it. In *A Global Affair*, he's a minor functionary who scoops up an abandoned foundling and fends off 111 determined countries, via their representatives, mostly female, all of whom want the child. Furthermore, the scenes of Mr. Hope and the little charmer have genuine appeal.

One of the writers of *A Global Affair*, Arthur Marx, is the son of Groucho Marx. He was later to co-author a few more Bob Hope films. Unfortunately, all are among the comedian's worst.

I'll Take Sweden

Directed by Frederick De Cordova. Screenplay by Bob Fisher and Arthur Marx. Story by Nat Perrin. Produced by Edward Small. Original Music by "By" Dunham, Jimmie Haskell, Ken Lauber, Bobby Beverly and Jim Economides. Cinematography by Daniel L. Fapp. Film Editing by Grant Whytock. Art Direction by Robert Peterson. Set Decoration by Frank Tuttle. Costume Design by Paula Giokaris. Stunts: Roger Creed and Jesse Wayne. Choreography by Miriam Nelson.

Cast: Bob Hope (Bob Holcomb); Tuesday Weld (JoJo Holcomb); Frankie Avalon (Kenny Klinger); Dina Merrill (Karin Granstedt); Jeremy Slate (Eric Carlson); Rosemarie Frankland (Marti); Walter Sande (Bjork); John Qualen (Olaf); Siv Marta Aberg (Inger); Peter Bourne (Ingemar); Fay DeWitt (Hilda); Alice Frost (Greta); Beverly Powers (Electra); Roy Roberts (Captain).

Released June 18, 1965, by United Artists.

I'll Take Sweden is Bob Hope's worst movie.

A generation gap comedy written by a handful of old men who were completely clueless about young people and the sexual revolution, *I'll Take Sweden* is such an utter embarrassment that it could very well develop a cult following along the same lines as Ed Wood's low-budget *Plan Nine from Outer Space* due to its many horrid elements.

The plot deals with Hope as Bob Holcomb, a conservative father who is naturally protective of his nubile young daughter JoJo (Tuesday Weld). He does not at all approve of her boyfriend (Frankie Avalon), a guitar-wielding slacker who appears to have no solid future.

Bob gets himself transferred to Sweden where his daughter meets a debonair playboy (Jeremy Slate), whose free thinking ideas about trial honeymoons and such make her American boyfriend seem better and better.

The film's co-scripter, Arthur Marx, had written an equally clueless play about the generation gap, *The Impossible Years*, which was also later made into a film. Surprisingly, the play won a Tony award, which shows just how

149

wide the actual generation gap was during the 1960s. The older adults had no idea of the youth culture and thus applauded plays and films that were completely off the track.

It is hard to fathom on how many levels *I'll Take Sweden* fails.

First, it represents a supreme lack of knowledge regarding what young people were thinking and feeling in 1965.

Casting twenty-six-year-old Frankie Avalon as a wayward teenager was outrageous. While Avalon is certainly a likable performer, he is hopelessly miscast here. The character of Kenny Klinger is supposed to be something of a threat to the staid father. Avalon was long noted as the clean-cut alternative to the more raucous rockers like Elvis Presley or Jerry Lee Lewis. To cast this sparkling, handsome man in the role of the rebellious 1960s teenager could only work as a parody.

Another one of the major problems with *I'll Take Sweden* is that it is not about Hope but about Weld. Hope's character is peripheral, and a subplot in which he falls for an interior decorator (Dina Merrill) almost seems like an intrusion.

Perhaps the funniest scene in the picture is a fantasy sequence in which Bob imagines his daughter married to the wayward youth, living in a trailer, and having to cope with abject poverty. It is silly, risqué for its time, and the only really amusing thing in the entire movie.

Arthur Marx is the son of Groucho, and the original story was penned by Nat Perrin, who had written for the Marx Brothers. However, that is where the similarity ends. Even the weakest Marx Brothers movie would be a far more enjoyable viewing experience than *I'll Take Sweden*.

Boy, Did I Get a Wrong Number!

Directed by George Marshall. Screenplay by George Kennett, Albert Lewin and Burt Styler. Story by George Beck. Produced by Edward Small. Original Music by "By" Dunham and Richard LaSalle. Cinematography by Lionel Lindon. Film Editing by Grant Whytock. Casting by Harvey Clermont. Art Direction by Frank Sylos. Set Decoration by H. Web Arrowsmith. Costume Design by Marjorie Corso. Makeup by Hal Lierley and Mike Moschella. Assistant Director: Herbert S. Greene. Art Department: Max Frankel. Sound by Alfred R. Bird, Edna Bullock and Clarence Peterson.

Cast: Bob Hope (Tom Meade); Elke Sommer (Didi); Phyllis Diller (Lily); Cesare Danova (Pepe Pepponi); Marjorie Lord (Martha Meade); Terry Burnham (Doris Meade); Kevin Burchett (Larry Meade); Kelly Thordsen (Schwartz); Benny Baker (Regan); Keith Taylor (Plympton); Harry von Zell (Newscaster); Joyce Jameson (Telephone Operator); John Todd Roberts (Newsboy).

Released June 30, 1966, by United Artists.

Boy, Did I Get a Wrong Number! has long held the reputation of being Hope's worst movie. This is, in part, based on Leonard Maltin's scathing comments in his popular book *TV Movies* in which he calls the film "absolutely painful."

Actually, *Boy, Did I Get a Wrong Number!* is generally rather amusing. It is not as bad as *Critic's Choice*, *I'll Take Sweden* or *Call Me Bwana*, but it is nowhere near his better films of the past.

Hope plays Tom Meade, a conservative real estate agent and family man, who gets misconnected by a switchboard operator to the hotel room of Dede (Elke Sommer), a Hollywood sexpot who has been reported missing. She talks Meade into bringing her some food and, eventually, hiding

Hope and Phyllis Diller in *Boy, Did I Get a Wrong Number!* (1966).

her out at his vacation cabin. When clues point to Meade's involvement with her, he soon finds himself accused of her murder.

One of the strong points of *Boy, Did I Get a Wrong Number!* is Phyllis Diller, as his housekeeper Lily. Diller was a wisecracking comedienne and therefore effective at trading quips with Hope. Lily has heard Meade's phone conversations with Dede via the extension and is recruited to help him out so that his wife (Marjorie Lord) does not discover his innocent dalliance and so he does not get arrested for murder.

It appears that the people behind *Boy, Did I Get a Wrong Number!*, including Hope himself, realized that at his age, he was best cast as the older, more conservative citizen whose quiet lifestyle was upset by events that were beyond his immediate world. His character of Tom Meade is generally representative of any staid sitcom father of the period. To throw him into a mix with a sexy film star and a supposed murder is the sort of tumult with which he cannot cope.

Hope's first appearance features real estate broker Tom Meade as jaunty and confident. As arrives home, he announces, "Sweetheart is here," and then mutters, "That oughta start an avalanche!" When Lily dismisses Mrs. Meade's going to a beauty parlor by stating, "I do my own hair," Tom Meade comments, "I was wondering where the eggbeater was." At one point his daughter looks at photos of a scantily clad Dede in the newspaper and comments, "how copious." Meade replies, "Watch your language." When later on the daughter's talk of sex and partial nudity in films annoys her mother, she looks to her husband for support and he states, "I'm still shocked by her using the word 'Copious'!"

Elke Sommer is quite good as the temperamental actress whose abilities as a thespian appear to be a succession of bathtub sequences meant to do little more than titillate her audience. The Meades do not allow their children to see Dede's films.

It should be noted that films of the 1960s sometimes look better now, decades later, than they did upon their initial release. Surrounded by the changes and innovations that were happening in movies at the time, *Boy, Did I Get a Wrong Number!* probably appeared corny and archaic. Now, with no timeframe to consider, *Boy, Did I Get a Wrong Number!* holds up as a pleasant, amusing farce with enough funny lines to help sustain the brisk pace.

It is rather interesting that the film acknowledges the greater freedoms in films of the period, based on American cinema's being influenced by much of what was happening in Europe. This greater creative freedom was a boon to maverick filmmakers, but it relegated films like *Boy, Did I Get a Wrong Number!* to older patrons who recalled Hope in his prime.

It may not have garnered any new fans for Bob Hope, but *Boy, Did I Get a Wrong Number!* is not as bad a film as its unfortunate reputation would have one believe. And, despite its limited audience demographic, it was a box office success.

8 on the Lam

Directed by George Marshall. Written by Bob Fisher, Albert Lewin, Arthur Marx and Burt Styler. Produced by Bill Lawrence. Original Music by George Romanis. Cinematography by Alan Stensvold. Film Editing by R. A. Radecki and Grant Whytock. Casting by Harvey Clermont. Art Direction by Walter M. Simonds. Set Decoration by Raymond Paul. Costume Design by Joseph Dimmitt and Marjorie Henderson. Makeup by Mike Moschella. Props by Monroe Liebgold. Sound by Alfred R. Bird, Audrey Granville, Al Overton and Clem Portman.

Cast: Bob Hope (Henry Dimsdale); Phyllis Diller (Golda); Jonathan Winters (Jasper Lynch); Shirley Eaton (Ellie Barton); Jill St. John (Monica); Stacey Maxwell (Linda); Kevin Brodie (Steve); Robert Hope (Mike); Glenn Gilger (Andy); Avis Hope (Dana); Debi Storm (Lois); Michael Freeman (Mark); Austin Willis (Mr. Pomeroy); Peter Leeds (Marty); Charles Lane (Bank Examiner); Herb Vigran (Real Estate Agent); Robert Foulk (Detective); Elvia Allman (Neighbor); Jonathan Hole (Salesman); Phil Arnold (Bald Man).

Released April 26, 1967, by United Artists.

Perhaps the box office success of *Boy, Did I Get a Wrong Number!* is the reason for *8 on the Lam,* which is another film in which Bob Hope plays a middle-class conservative who gets mixed up with a serious criminal act.

Hope is Henry Dimsdale, a widowed bank teller with seven children and a housekeeper, Golda (Phyllis Diller). He finds $10,000 in cash, part of which he uses to buy a new car. His colleagues are surprised at his new-found wealth, but when his books show a $50,000 shortage, he is believed to have embezzled it from the bank. He flees with his seven children, trying desperately to clear himself while the cops are after him. Golda's boyfriend, a detective (Jonathan Winters), is leading the pursuit, so Golda tries to throw him off the track until Henry can prove his innocence.

While not as bad as *I'll Take Sweden,* this is still one of Hope's lesser films and is indicative of this lackluster period of his film career. Apparently

the idea was to veer from the more mature content of *Boy, Did I Get a Wrong Number!* and move more toward the lucrative family trade. Throwing in a gaggle of kids helps a film with older stars appeal to the younger set.

On that level it is amusing in the fashion of a sitcom, and, like most movies from this very strange period of film history, is considered an interesting time capsule due to the funky furniture and clothing styles that were popular in 1967.

The cast is strong. Both Hope and Diller have their share of funny lines, but they have less screen time together than in *Boy, Did I Get a Wrong Number!*

Jonathan Winters appears to enjoy mugging it up as a self-important detective, especially appearing with Diller as his obtrusive girlfriend.

Jill St. John and Shirley Eaton, two very attractive actresses from the period, do well in their decidedly limited roles.

Rounding out the small parts with familiar faces like Peter Leeds, Elvia Allman, Phil Arnold, Herb Vigran, and Charles Lane helps bolster the film's retro-nostalgic appeal.

8 on the Lam is not a film that holds up well, however, even as an offbeat cultural artifact. It ends with a slapstick chase sequence, as did *Boy, Did I Get a Wrong Number!*. Both were directed by veteran George Marshall, whose career of over one hundred films lasted from early silent movies to 1970s television. Marshall had also helmed such Hope films as *The Ghost Breakers*, *Monsieur Beaucaire*, and *Off Limits* as well as some of the better Laurel and Hardy and Martin and Lewis pictures.

It is unfortunate that all of the talent and good intentions that went into the making of *8 on the Lam* did not result in a better movie.

Opposite page: Ad for *8 on the Lam*, 1967.

The Private Navy
of Sergeant O'Farrell

Directed by Frank Tashlin. Written by Robert M. Fresco, John L. Greene and Frank Tashlin. Produced by John Beck. Original Music by Harry Sukman. Cinematography by Alan Stensvold. Film Editing by Eda Warren. Art Direction by Robert Kinoshita. Set Decoration by Fred Price. Costume Design by Oscar Rodriguez. Makeup by Mike Moschella. Assistant Director: Kurt Neumann. Sound by John Caper, Jr., Harold Lewis and Clem Portman.

Cast: Bob Hope (Sgt. Dan O'Farrell); Phyllis Diller (Nellie Krause); Jeffrey Hunter (Lt. Lyman P. Jones); Mylène Demongeot (Gaby); Gina Lollobrigida (Maria); John Myhers (Lt. Cdr. Roger Snavely); Mako Calvin (Coolidge Ishimura); Henry Wilcoxon (R. Adm. Arthur L. Stokes); Dick Sargent (Capt. Elwood Prohaska); Christopher Dark (Pvt. George Strongbow); Michael Burns (Pvt. Johnny Bannon); William Wellman, Jr. (Cpl. Kennedy); Robert Donner (Pvt. Ogg [Marine]); Jack Grinnage (Pvt. Roberts); William Christopher (Pvt. Jack Schultz); John Spina (Corporal Miller).

Released May 8, 1968, by United Artists.

The Private Navy of Sergeant O'Farrell likely appeared out of sync at the time of its initial release, and it has dated even further in the ensuing decades.

Hope plays O'Farrell, who is stuck on a South Pacific island that has been overlooked by the war. When a cargo ship full of beer is torpedoed, O'Farrell tries to get the liquor to his troops in order to boost morale. He also tries to get some women on the island but ends up with Phyllis Diller.

It is surprising that *The Private Navy of Sergeant O'Farrell* was directed by Frank Tashlin. Tashlin had worked well with Hope in the past, first offering reshot scenes to improve the quality of *Monsieur Beaucaire* and then providing the wild slapstick chase climax to *My Favorite Brunette*. His direction of *Son of Paleface* is one of the reasons why it is one of Hope's best films.

Tashlin became a darling of French directors like Jean Luc Godard and Francois Truffaut for such films as *Will Success Spoil Rock Hunter* and *Hollywood or Bust*, which effectively satirize showbiz glitz.

The Private Navy of Sergeant O'Farrell is neither amusing nor inspired. It is a dull comedy that limps along with throwaway lines and uneventful sequences.

While some Hope films now appear a bit better than they did at the time of their initial release, *The Private Navy of Sergeant O'Farrell* is a Hope movie that is best avoided, even all these years later.

How to Commit Marriage

Directed by Norman Panama. Writing Credits: Michael Kanin and Ben Starr. Original Music by Joseph J. Lilley. Cinematography by Charles Lang. Film Editing by Ronald Sinclair. Art Direction by Edward D. Engoron. Set Decoration by John Lamphear. Costume Design by Nolan Miller. Makeup by Mike Moschella and Fred Williams. Special Effects by Justus Gibbs.

Cast: Bob Hope (Frank Benson); Jackie Gleason (Oliver Poe); Jane Wyman (Elaine Benson); Maureen Arthur (Lois Grey); JoAnna Cameron (Nancy Benson); Tim Matheson (David Poe); Leslie Nielsen (Phil Fletcher); Tina Louise (Laverne Baker); Paul Stewart (Willoughby); Irwin Corey (The Baba Ziba).

Released July 7, 1969, by Cinerama.

How to Commit Marriage is another attempt by Hope and his people to become relevant in the ever-changing cinematic landscape of the 1960s. Unfortunately, this tired generation gap farce appeared dated at the time of its initial release. Now it can only be embraced as camp.

Hope plays Frank Benson, a staid middle-class father who is going through a divorce. When his daughter reacts to the divorce by choosing to live out of wedlock with her boyfriend, it raises her father's ire. The boy's father (Jackie Gleason) is a record producer who has a more progressive attitude about the relationship. When the daughter has a baby and gives it up for adoption, her parents adopt it, adding further stress to their already difficult relationship.

It seems almost criminal that a film that co-stars Bob Hope and Jackie Gleason should be a misfire, but *How to Commit Marriage* certainly is.

As with Hope's even less effective generation gap comedy *I'll Take Sweden*, *How to Commit Marriage* was clearly written by older people who had only the most cursory knowledge of the youthful revolution that permeated 1960s pop culture so completely. The best they could do was make jokes about group names or offer Hope stale one-liners about the generation gap that are far beneath his talent.

It had gotten to the point where Hope's films were now as dull as his concurrent TV specials. At once among the most popular and relevant comedians on the scene, Bob Hope was now among the most tiresome. Although *How to Commit Marriage* did turn a profit, due likely to its heavyweight cast, it became difficult for Hope to secure another movie deal.

Cancel My Reservation

Directed by Paul Bogart. Screenplay by Bob Fisher and Arthur Marx. Based on the novel *The Broken Gun* by Louis L'Amour. Produced by Bob Hope and Gordon Oliver. Original Music by Dominic Frontiere. Cinematography by Russell Metty. Film Editing by Michael A. Hoey. Art Direction by Rolland M. Brooks. Set Decoration by Anthony Mondell. Sound by Dan Wallin.

Cast: Bob Hope (Dan Bartlett); Eva Marie Saint (Sheila Bartlett); Ralph Bellamy (John Ed); Forrest Tucker (Reese); Anne Archer (Crazy Hollister); Keenan Wynn (Sheriff Riley); Henry Darrow (Joe Little Cloud); Chief Dan George (Old Bear); Doodles Weaver (Cactus); Betty Carr (Mary Little Cloud); Herb Vigran (Snagby); Pat Morita (Yamamoto); Gordon Oliver (Mr. Sparker); Isabella Hoopes (Elderly Lady); Buster Schaefer (Doc Morton); Tracy Bogart and Trudy Bordoff (Teenage Girls); Richard Yniguez and Priscilla Garcia (Motorcyclists); Johnny Carson, Bing Crosby, John Wayne and Flip Wilson (as themselves).

Released September 21, 1972, by Warner Brothers.

Hope acquired the rights to a Louis L'Amour western book entitled *The Broken Gun.* He planned for Hope Enterprises to make a serious western with another actor appearing as the lead. The project didn't get off the ground, so he decided to have some writers transform the book into a comedy starring himself, so as not to have wasted the money acquiring the rights.

Writers Bob Fischer and Arthur Marx were recruited to transform the novel into a comedy screenplay for Hope. They had a weak record with the comedian, having been involved in some of his worst films including *8 on the Lam* and *I'll Take Sweden.*

Both writers agreed that the L'Amour novel was not constructed for comedy and asked if they could simply write an original comedy screenplay for Hope. Hope, however, wanted them to make something out of the novel, so Marx and Fischer did their best to transform a heavy western into a light comedy.

The novel about Indian reservations and murder was turned into a lightweight vehicle with Hope appearing as a talk show host who heads west with his wife in order to save their faltering marriage. Their cabin in Arizona happens to be on land that an Indian tribe has claimed as their own. When an Indian girl is murdered, the talk show host is blamed.

Hope liked the reworking of the novel and set out to act as the film's producer. He landed a release deal with Warner Brothers, but only under the condition that he hire a younger director with more contemporary ideas rather than an old timer like George Marshall. Hope agreed, and Paul Bogart was hired.

Bogart was not exactly young. He was past fifty and a World War II veteran, but his style was in keeping with the more contemporary methods of Mel Brooks or Woody Allen in that his most-noted work had been helming the innovative television series "All in the Family," for which Marx had done some writing.

Bogart liked the idea of directing a Bob Hope movie, with its breezy style and the funny lines. Recalling the old Bob Hope classics, he felt he could put together a fun movie in the Hope vein.

However, Bogart was incensed at the way Hope handled his role as producer. Apparently Hope had misgivings about a straight comedy script and kept having his myriad writers add jokes. Also, Hope's old-fashioned ideas clashed with anything progressive that Bogart wanted to try. As the film's producer and star, Hope had the last word.

What is most interesting, perhaps, about *Cancel My Reservation* is its old-fashioned, corny style. It seems like a group of people satirizing the lesser aspects of a Bob Hope film from this period.

Cancel My Reservation was booked into the massive Radio City Music Hall in New York City. It was the first Bob Hope film to play there. The world's largest movie theater had less than three hundred people in attendance for the premiere of *Cancel My Reservation*. It received sporadic release, was poorly attended throughout the country, and lost money.

Cancel My Reservation was Bob Hope's final starring film.

The Road Picture
That Never Was

In 1976, Hope announced that he, Bing Crosby, and Dorothy Lamour would reunite for one more Road picture. The film was to be called *The Road to Tomorrow*, and would be penned by Ben Starr, who had written for Hope before.

Preparations were slow but steady. It was planned to have Hope, Crosby, and Lamour play grandparents. They all heartily agreed, and Crosby and Hope even paid for the option themselves. However, they did ask to change the title to *The Road to the Fountain of Youth*.

The story would have Hope, Crosby, and Lamour run into each other at an airport where they had come with their respective grandchildren to embark on European vacations. Of course they end up on the same plane and involved in a mystery.

Bing Crosby, Dorothy Lamour and Hope announcing *A New Road* (1976).

Plans for this Road picture were suspended when Bing was seriously injured in a fall into an orchestra pit from a stage that was twenty feet high. His recovery was complete but slow.

Just as soon as Crosby was well enough to go back to work, plans continued for shooting *The Road to the Fountain of Youth* in the fall of 1977.

On October 14, 1977, Bing Crosby was appearing at a golf tournament at the La Moralejo Golf Club outside of Madrid, Spain. As he prepared to tee off on the eighteenth hole, Crosby fell to the ground with a massive heart attack. He died on the way to the hospital.

Hope was on tour at the time of Bing's death and was told the news by telephone. He canceled his next several appearances and flew back to his home in Burbank, California, by private jet. He remained in seclusion until the funeral. Although Crosby's will indicated that the funeral should be a private affair for the family, his widow invited his closest friends, including Hope and his wife.

Hope stated:

> The whole world loved Bing with a devotion that not only crossed international boundaries but erased them. He made the world a single place through his music, spoke to it in a language that everybody understands — the language of the heart.

b

Appendix A:
Hope's Cameo Appearances

Bob Hope made guest appearances in a handful of films over the years. Sometimes he would simply appear as himself; other times he would make an amusing cameo or an uncredited surprise appearance.

Star Spangled Rhythm (1942)
This is a musical review with an all-star cast, in which Hope appears as himself, with Jerry Colonna.

The Story of G.I. Joe (1945)
In this story about journalist Ernie Pyle, Hope provides his own voice as part of the film's narration. Burgess Meredith starred in the title role as Pyle, whose wartime correspondence was very popular until he was shot and killed while on duty.

Variety Girl (1947)
This is another Paramount all-star production in which several of the studios stars appear. The plot deals with an abandoned baby found by some producers and sponsored by the Variety Guild of America. When she becomes a teenager, she returns to the studio in hopes of stardom. Broadway musical star Mary Hatcher had the title role. While she had little success in films, appearing in B pictures like *The Big Wheel, Isn't It Romantic,* and *Holiday in Havana,* Ms. Hatcher was quite a star on Broadway, originating the female lead in the production of "Oklahoma." Hope and Bing Crosby have a very funny bit on the Paramount studio lot:

> BOB: I was talking to the head of the studio today.
> BING: Why, was he squawking about how you've been doing the laundry?

Ad for *Variety Girl*, 1947.

BOB: How's your golf?
BING: Oh, I'm in my seventies.
BOB: Yeah, I know, but how's your golf?

The puppetoon sequence in the original release was shown in color, but on TV and video it has always been shown in black and white.

The Greatest Show on Earth (1952)

In Cecil B. DeMille's Oscar winning feature about circus life, there is a shot of the audience. As the camera pans the spectators, we see Bing Crosby and Bob Hope sitting among them. Bing and Bob shot this while on break from filming *Road to Bali*.

Scared Stiff (1953)

In Dean Martin and Jerry Lewis's remake of Hope's 1940 feature *The Ghost Breakers*, the final scene features an amusing cameo by Hope and Crosby.

The Five Pennies (1959)

Hope does a brief cameo in this biographical musical about Red Nichols, played by Danny Kaye.

Showdown at Ulcer Gulch (1956)

This is an interesting pastiche with appearances by Hope, Crosby, Ernie Kovacs, Edie Adams, and Groucho and Chico Marx. It was directed by Disney animator Shamus Culhane, who was Chico Marx's son-in-law.

Not with My Wife, You Don't! (1966)

Hope makes another brief appearance in this tired romantic farce featuring Tony Curtis.

The Oscar (1966)

In this bloated drama about the Academy Awards, Hope appears as himself hosting the Oscar telecast.

Hope also made appearances in the following short films:

Don't Hook Now (1938)
Screen Snapshots Series 19, No. 6 (1940)
Hedda Hopper's Hollywood No. 4 (1942)
Strictly G.I. (1943)
Combat America (1943)
Show Business at War (1943)
The All-Star Bond Rally (1945)
Hollywood Victory Caravan (1945)
Screen Actors (1950)
Screen Snapshots: Memorial to Al Jolson (1952)
Screen Snapshots: Hollywood's Invisible Man (1954)
Screen Snapshots: Hollywood Beauty (1955)
Screen Snapshots: Hollywood Star Night (1957)

Appendix B:
Hope on Radio

Hope has stated that it was his popularity on radio that helped him rise from Harold Hurley's B-picture unit at Paramount to the more prestigious A pictures like *The Cat and the Canary* and *The Ghost Breakers* that helped his film career.

Radio began in 1919 and within the next five years there were over three million radio sets in households across America. By 1930, the broadcast system was fairly well established, and networks were eager to fill airtime with interesting personalities.

Hope did some sporadic radio work, usually as a wisecracking host as per his vaudeville emcee duties.

In 1938, NBC studios asked if he would like to star in a series sponsored by Pepsodent toothpaste. Hope agreed and set out to find the best comedy writers available. He also suggested the hit song "Thanks for the Memory" as his theme song.

Hope acquired the services of a few regulars, including announcer Bill Goodwin, bandleader Skinnay Ennis, comedians Jerry Colonna and Vera Vague (Barbara Jo Allen), actresses Elvia Allman and Blanche Stewart as Brenda and Cobina, and the singing group Six Hits and a Miss.

The show premiered on Tuesday night, September 27, 1938. It was not an immediate hit. In fact, there were nearly two months of weekly broadcasts before "The Pepsodent Show" hit its stride.

Hope often credits the catch phrases of Jerry Colonna for helping to secure a steady audience. Colonna always greeted people as "gate." His opening line, "Greetings Gate" became a popular phrase, and such things helped bolster Hope's ratings. In the jargon of the period, a "gate" was a person who could swing.

Judy Garland was a regular on the show for over a year and worked exceptionally well with Hope. Not only did she do well as a singer but her

Hope with Bing Crosby during a radio performance.

natural timing allowed her to participate in the comedy sketches as well. Other popular female singers who appeared as regulars include Frances Langford, Doris Day, and Gloria Jean.

Hope's show was unique at the time but can now be understood as a milestone in that it was the first true variety show. It opened with his monologue and then was filled with comedy sketches, musical numbers, and a general sense of breezy fun that helped bolster the comedian's career greatly.

"The Pepsodent Show" made Hope a household name. By the end of the year, he was ranked fourth among radio's comedians. By 1940, he had moved up to first place, edging out such radio stalwarts as Jack Benny and Fred Allen.

The pace of Hope's radio show was brisk and filled with jokes. At one point his program was clocked at having seven jokes per minute!

Most of the comedy was give-and-take, the sort of repartee that was quite popular during this period. Of course by today's standards it may seem corny, but it is the sort of old-fashioned fun that causes us to laugh in spite of ourselves:

> HOPE: I did really well in my tennis match against Mickey Rooney.
> JUDY GARLAND: That was exciting!
> HOPE: I smashed the ball as hard as I could. Mickey smashed it right back. Boy can he hit! He drove it so hard, when it stopped bouncing the ball said, "Listen fellers can't we settle this thing some other way?"

Hope on radio.

This silliness was just the thing for homebound audiences tuned in to their radios. It made them aware of Hope and his style of breezy comedy. It also generated interest in his movies.

Hope's success on radio kept building and helped secure him better parts in films at Paramount by the following year, when he made *The Cat and the Canary*. In 1939, he was asked to emcee the Academy Awards ceremonies, which he did for the next several decades. 1939 was the year of *Gone with the Wind*, produced by David O. Selznick. It was nominated in so many categories, Hope opened the awards show by stating, "This is really nice, this party for Selznick."

By 1947, Hope was among the top box office stars in movies, but critics were beginning to pan his radio show for "sameness." Audiences started dropping off, too. In 1949 his ratings were 23.8, by 1951 they were 12.7, and by 1953 they were only 5.4. Of course television had, by then, become established and radio was dying out. Music programming had taken over by the mid–1950s, and near the end of that decade, Hope ended his radio show.

Radio made Bob Hope a star. Thus, the radio work of Bob Hope likely deserves a book of its own. However, it was also instrumental in securing better film work for him and, as a result, deserves some discussion in a book about his movies.

Appendix C:
Hope on Television

As with his radio career, a separate book on Hope's television career is certainly needed. This listing of his television work is a thumbnail guide to his work on the small screen. PC stands for production code.

Initially, it should be noted that Hope appeared on the first commercial broadcast in the West in January of 1947:

> This is Bob "first commercial television broadcast" Hope, telling you gals who have tuned me in — and I wanna make this emphatic — if my face isn't handsome and debonair, it isn't me it's the static.
>
> Here it is 1947 and we're holding the first commercial television broadcast in the west. Commercial — what a lovely word. Up until tonight, I looked at television as something I might dabble in for a night or so. A week. Maybe a month. But now that's it's gone commercial, meet "The Yearling."

Television Appearances

Toast of the Town (1950); Hope does an eight-minute comedy monologue.

Frigidaire's Star Spangled Review (1950), appearing as host

What's My Line? (1951), appearing as Mystery Guest

The Colgate Comedy Hour, TV series (guest host, 1952 to 1953)

The Bob Hope Show (1952) TV series

The 25th Annual Academy Awards (1953)

The Jack Benny Program, appearing as himself in episode "Goldie, Fields and Glide" (episode 4.10) first telecast March 21, 1954

The Jack Benny Program, appearing as himself in episode "The Road to Nairobi" (episode 4.13) first telecast May 23, 1954

Bing Crosby and Hope re-create their old pat-a-cake bit on one of Bob's television specials with Dorothy Lamour.

Colgate Comedy Hour (1950) appearing as Huckleberry Haines in episode "Roberta," recreating his Broadway sensation of fifteen years earlier. Broadcast on April 10, 1955

The 27th Annual Academy Awards (1955); himself/host

I Love Lucy, appearing as himself in episode: "Lucy and Bob Hope" (episode 6.1) first telecast October 1, 1956, and in reruns ever since. Hope briefly plugs his current film, *The Iron Petticoat.*

The Jack Benny Program, appearing as himself in episode "Hope and Benny in Agent's Office" (episode 7.12) first telecast February 24, 1957

The Frank Sinatra Show (1957), appearing as himself (episode 1.1) October 18, 1957

The 30th Annual Academy Awards (1958); co-host

The Jack Benny Program, appearing as himself in episode "Stars' Wives Show" (episode 9.4) November 2, 1958

The 31st Annual Academy Awards (1959); co-host

Frances Langford Presents (1959) TV series; himself

The 32nd Annual Academy Awards (1960); host/Hersholt Award Recipient

The 33rd Annual Academy Awards (1961); host

The Bing Crosby Show (1961); himself ... aka Bing Crosby in London (1961) (USA)

The Jack Benny Program, appearing as himself in episode "The Bob Hope Show" (episode 13.10) December 4, 1962

Bob Hope Presents the Chrysler Theatre (1963) TV series; host (also broadcast as *The Chrysler Theater*) and released to syndication as *Universal Star Time*. In this anthology series, dramatic stories were presented by Hope. These dramas featured some of the top actors, writers, and directors active in television at the time. There were many anthology series during the 1950s and 1960s. This was one of the best. A list of episodes from its four seasons follows:

Chrysler Theatre Season 1

1. "A Killing at Sundial," starring Stuart Whitman, Angie Dickinson, Melvyn Douglas. Broadcast October 4, 1963; written by Rod Serling; directed by Alex Segal.

2. "Something About Lee Wiley," starring Piper Laurie (Lee Wiley), Claude Rains, Steven Hill, Alfred Ryder. Broadcast October 11, 1963; directed by Sydney Pollack, who received an Emmy nomination for this episode.

3. "Seven Miles of Bad Road," starring Jeffrey Hunter (Gabe Flanders), Eleanor Parker, Neville Brand. Broadcast October 18, 1963; written by Douglas Heyes; directed by Douglas Heyes.

4. "Four Kings," starring Peter Falk, Susan Strasberg, John van Dreelen (Colonel Nauman), Simon Oakland, Paul Lukas, Robert Strauss, Vito Scotti, Than Wyenn, Eric Braeden (listed as Hans Gudegast in the film credits). Broadcast October 18, 1963.

5. "One Day in the Life of Ivan Denisovich," starring Jason Robards, Jr. (Ivan Denisovich), Harold J. Stone (Turin), Albert Paulsen (Lt. Volkovoi), Hurd Hatfield (Tsezar), Torin Thatcher (Buinovsky), John Fiedler, Mike Kellin (Kilgas), George Kennedy, John Abbot, Curt Conway (Fetukov), Rodolfo Acosta. Broadcast November 8, 1963; written by Mark Rodgers; original story by Alexander Solzhenitsyn; directed by Dan Petrie. Albert Paulsen won an Emmy for Best Supporting Actor for his performance in this episode.

6. "The House Next Door." Broadcast November 15, 1963; starring Bing Crosby.

7. "The Fifth Passenger." Broadcast November 29, 1963. This episode was preempted due to the assassination of John F. Kennedy.

8. "The Candidate," starring Milton Berle, Dina Merrill, Ruth Roman, Robert Webber, Hope Holiday, J. D. Cannon, Simon Scott, John McLiam, James Flavin, Isabelle Cooley, Jay Adler, Davis Roberts, John Francis. Broadcast December 6, 1963; written by Karl Miller; original story by Eugene Burdick; directed by Stuart Rosenberg.

9. "It's Mental Work," starring Gena Rowlands (June), Lee J. Cobb (Ernie Wigman), Harry Guardino (Rich), Stanley Adams (Vito Conte), Mary Wickes (Nurse), George N. Neise (John), Archie Moore (Buddy). Broadcast December 20, 1963; written by Rod Serling; original story by John O'Hara; directed by Alex North. The teleplay for this episode (an adaptation of a John O'Hara story) won Rod Serling an Emmy for Outstanding Writing Achievement in Drama, Adaptation (1963–1964).

10. "Corridor 400," starring Suzanne Pleshette (Anita King), Andrew Duggan, Theodore Bikel, Joseph Campanella, Frank Overton. Broadcast date December 27, 1963. This was an unsold pilot for Pleshette.

11. "War of Nerves," starring Louis Jourdan, Stephen Boyd, Emile Genest, Monique Le Marie. Broadcast January 3, 1964.

12. "Runaway," starring Hugh O'Brien (Richie Darden), Joey Heatherton (Cress), Keenan Wynn (Mig Semple), Berkeley Harris, Ellen Burstyn, John Alderman, Nancy Ames, Donna Anderson, Jeff Cooper. Broadcast January 10, 1964; written by Leonard Kantor; original story by Thomas B. Dewey; directed by Paul Stewart.

13. "The Seven Little Foys," starring Mickey Rooney (George M. Cohan), Eddie Foy, Jr. (Eddie Foy), the Osmond Brothers, Elaine Edwards, George Tobias, Naomi Stevens, Betty Bronson. Broadcast January 24, 1964. Based on the 1955 movie *The Seven Little Foys*. This was also a proposed television series.

14. "Two Is the Number," starring Shelley Winters (Jenny Dworak), Martin Balsam, David Opatoshu, Mike Kellin, Joseph Mell, George Voskovec. Broadcast date January 31, 1964; written by Franklin Barton; directed by Sidney Pollack. Winters won an Emmy for Best Dramatic Actress in this role.

15. "A Wind of Hurricane Force," starring Dana Andrews, Joe De Santis, Marisa Pavan, Tony Musante. Broadcast February 7, 1964.

16. "Wake Up Darling," starring Roddy McDowall (Deerfield Prescott), Barry Nelson (Don Emerson), Janet Blair (Polly Emerson), Ann B. Davis (Juliet), Joyce Jameson (Gloria). Broadcast February 21, 1964; written by Alex Gottlieb.

17. "Meal Ticket," broadcast February 28, 1964.

18. "The Square Peg," broadcast March 6, 1964. This episode was rescheduled from November 22, 1963, the day President John F. Kennedy was assassinated, to March 6, 1964.

19. "White Snow, Red Ice," starring Senta Berger (Mia), Jack Kelly (Frederick Piper), Walter Matthau (Tom Gregory), George Petrie (Director), Grace Lee Whitney (Mona), Francine York (Actress). Broadcast March 13, 1964.

20. "Her School for Bachelors," starring Eva Marie Saint, Francine York. Broadcast March 20, 1964.

21. "A Slow Fade to Black," starring Rod Steiger (Mike Kirsch), Robert Culp, James Dunn (Landers), Anna Lee, Sally Kellerman, Dabney Coleman, Michael Pataki (Young Mike Kirsch). Broadcast March 27, 1964; pc: 24040; written by Steven Bochco, Rod Serling; directed by Joseph Leytes, Roy Winston. "A Slow Fade to Black" was turned into a movie called *The Movie Maker*. To pad the running time to two hours, Universal filmed a series of flashback sequences set in the 1920s. Steven Bochco scripted the latter half and Joseph Leytes directed.

22. "A Case of Armed Robbery," starring Pat O'Brien (Otto Mead), Anthony Franciosa (Jack Montrose), Bethel Leslie (Jean Rice), Paul Stewart (Alfred), Lisabeth Hush (Carol), Russell Thorsen (Ganoulian), Kevin Tate (Danny), Edward Asner, Steve Ihnat. Broadcast April 3, 1964; written by Franklin Barton; directed by Herschel Daugherty.

23. "Time for Elizabeth," starring Groucho Marx (Ed Davis), Eden Marx (Vivian Morgan), Roland Winters (Walter Schaeffer), Kathryn Eames (Kay Davis), Carole Wells (Anne), John Considine (Richard Coburn). Broadcast April 24, 1964; written by Groucho Marx, Norman Krasna.

24. "The Game with Glass Pieces," starring Darren McGavin, George Peppard. Broadcast May 1, 1964.

25. "The Command," starring Robert Stack. Broadcast May 22, 1964; pc: 24049; written by Rod Serling; directed by Fielder Cook.

26. "The Sojourner," starring Efrem Zimbalist, Jr. (John Ferris), Vera Miles, Herschel Bernardi, Howard Duff, Ellen Corby, Warren Stevens, Torin Thatcher, Chana Eden. Broadcast May 29, 1964; written by Stirling Silliphant; original story by Carson McCullers; directed by Stuart Rosenberg.

27. "Echo of Evil," starring Joan Hackett, John Saxon, Jane Wyatt, Barry Sullivan (Oscar Teckla), Nehemiah Persoff. Broadcast June 5, 1964.

CHRYSLER THEATRE SEASON 2

28. "Think Pretty," starring Fred Astaire, Barrie Chase, Louis Nye, Jean Hersholt, Reta Shaw. Broadcast October 2, 1964.

29. "Murder in the First," starring Janet Leigh (Carol Hartley), Bobby Darin (Brad Kubec), Lloyd Bochner. Broadcast October 9, 1964.

30. "Have Girls Will Travel," starring Lucille Ball, Jill St. John, Rhonda Fleming, Rod Cameron, Aldo Ray, Marilyn Maxwell. Broadcast October 16, 1964.

31. "The Turncoat," starring Margaret O'Brien, George Hamilton (Peter Thornton), Carroll O'Connor, Jack Weston, Rodolfo Acosta, Jerry Douglas, Don Marshall, Peggy Ward, Dick Wilson, Frank Evans. Broadcast October 23, 1964; written by Mark Rodgers, John Joseph; directed by Ron Winston.

32. "The Timothy Heist," starring Art Carney, Spring Byington, Reginald Denny, Ted Cassidy. Broadcast October 30, 1964; written by Philip Davis, David Davis; original story by John Haase.

33. "Out of the Outskirts of Town," broadcast November 6, 1964.

34. "Parties to the Crime," starring Jeffrey Hunter (Barry Stinson), Sally Kellerman, Darren McGavin. Broadcast November 27, 1964.

35. "Mr. Biddle's Crime Wave," starring Roddy McDowall (Arthur Biddle), Shari Lewis, Pat Crowley, Lloyd Nolan, Willard Waterman, Parley Baer, George N. Neise, Joseph Mell, John Considine. Broadcast December 4, 1964; written by Nathaniel Curtis; directed by Lawrence Dobkin.

36. "The Shattered Glass," starring Shirley Jones, William Shatner, Dan O'Herlihy. Broadcast December 11, 1964.

37. "The Clash of Cymbals," starring Jack Klugman, Louis Jourdan, Laura Devon (Laura Macon), John Bleifer, Torben Meyer, Antony Eustrel, Bea Silvern. Broadcast December 25, 1964; written by Elick Moll; directed by Robert Ellis Miller.

38. "Double Jeopardy," starring Lauren Bacall, Jack Kelly, Lee Meriwether, Tom Poston, Diane McBain, Jean Hale, Hugh O'Brian (Fred Piper), Zsa Zsa Gabor. Broadcast January 8, 1965.

39. "Exit from a Plane Flight," starring Lloyd Bridges, Hugh O'Brian. Broadcast January 22, 1965; pc: 25532; written by Rod Serling. This episode was also known as "A Certain Sky Revisited."

40. "The Loving Cup," starring Lee Marvin, Polly Bergen, Patrick O'Neal, Peter Adams. Broadcast January 29, 1965.

41. "The Fliers," starring John Cassavetes, Carol Lynley, Chester Morris. Broadcast February 5, 1965; pc: 25516; written by David Rayfield; directed by Sydney Pollack.

42. "Cops and Robbers," starring Claude Rains, Bert Lahr, Eduardo Ciannelli, John Qualen, Ken Murray, Billy De Wolfe. Broadcast February 19, 1965.

43. "Terror Island," starring Ginger Rogers, Carol Lawrence, Katharine Ross, Donnelly Rhodes, Abraham Sofaer, William Fawcett, Jon Locke, Jeannine Fetterolf. Broadcast February 26, 1965; pc: 25547; written by Chester Krumholz; directed by John Brahm.

44. "The War and Eric Kurtz," starring Warren Oates, Martin Milner, Lloyd Bochner, Jack Ging (Major MacAlister), Don Marshall. Broadcast March 5, 1965 pc: 25557.

45. "In Any Language," starring John Forsythe (King), Ricardo Montalban (Aldo Carmenelli), Nanette Fabray (Hannah King), Ed Hashim, Mabel Albertson, Jean Hale, Leon Belasco, Al Ruscio, Rolfe Sedan, Penny Stanton, John Aniston. Broadcast March 12, 1965; written by Henry Garson, Edmund Beloin; directed by Lawrence Dobkin.

46. "Perilous Times," starring Peter Falk, Diane Baker. Broadcast March 19, 1965; pc: 25560.

47. "Memorandum for a Spy [1]," starring Robert Stack (James Andrew Congers), Victor Buono (Leo Khareet), John van Dreelen (Strellin), Felicia Farr (Jemy), Albert Paulsen (Avatin), Michael Constantine (Niri), George Macready (Graham Jutland), J. D. Cannon (Dr. Webb), Don Gordon (Harry Edmunds), Vincent Gardenia, Martin Milner, Leon Belasco (Gregor), John Hoyt (Lowell Ritchards), Danielle Aubry. Broadcast April 2, 1965; written by Robert L. Joseph; directed by Stuart Rosenberg. This episode was also released as a TV movie under the title of *Asylum for a Spy*.

48. "Memorandum for a Spy [2]," starring Robert Stack (James Andrew Congers), Victor Buono (Leo Khareet), John van Dreelen (Strellin,) Felicia Farr (Jemy), Albert Paulsen (Avatin), Michael Constantine (Niri), George Macready (Graham Jutland), J. D. Cannon (Dr. Webb), Don Gordon (Harry Edmunds), Vincent Gardenia, Martin Milner, Leon Belasco (Gregor), John Hoyt (Lowell

Ritchards), Danielle Aubry, Berry Kroeger. Broadcast April 9, 1965; written by Robert L. Joseph; directed by Stuart Rosenberg.

49. "A Time for Killing," starring Michael Parks, Dale Evans. Broadcast April 30, 1965; pc: 25545; written by Edward Anhalt; original story by William Hardy.

50. "Escape Into Jeopardy," starring James Franciscus (Larry Martin), Jocelyn Lane, Leif Erickson, Werner Klemperer, Gregory Morton, Joe De Santis, Tony Musante. Broadcast May 28, 1965; pc: 25554.

51. "Simon Says Get Married," starring Dorothy Provine, Martin Milner (Stanley Patrick), Bob Newhart, Joanna Barnes. Broadcast June 4, 1965.

CHRYSLER THEATRE SEASON 3

52. "The Game," starring Cliff Robertson, Maurice Evans. Broadcast September 15, 1965; written by S. Lee Pogostin; directed by Sydney Pollack. Cliff Robertson won an Emmy for his portrayal. Sydney Pollack won an Emmy for directing this episode.

53. "The Crime," starring Jack Lord (DA Abraham Lincoln Perez), Dana Wynter (Sarah Rodman), Pat O'Brien, Sheree North, Berkeley Harris, Karen Steele, Bill Quinn, Melodie Johnson, Walter Woolf King, Michael Pataki. Broadcast September 22, 1965; pc: 25562; written by Mark Rodgers; original story by Stephen Longstreet; directed by Ron Winston.

54. "March from Camp Tyler," starring Peter Lawford, Bethel Leslie. Broadcast date October 6, 1965.

55. "Kicks," starring Mickey Rooney, Jack Weston, Melodie Johnson, Harold J. Stone, Don Gordon. Broadcast October 13, 1965.

56. "Back to Back," starring Shelley Winters (Edith), Jack Hawkins, Shirley Grayson. Broadcast October 27, 1965; pc: 25561; written by David Rayfiel; original story by Elizabeth Taylor.

57. "Mister Governess," starring Carol Lawrence, Tom Tryon, Jacques Bergerac, Robert Clary, Alice Backes, Fred Clark, Suzie Kay, Mark Winters, Michael Blake. Broadcast November 10, 1965.

58. "Russian Roulette," starring Don Rickles, Jill St. John, Leon Askin, Victor Buono, Bob Hope. Broadcast November 17, 1965.

59. "Highest Fall of All," starring Stuart Whitman, Joan Hackett, Gary Merrill, Terry Moore, Robert Q. Lewis. Broadcast December 1, 1965.

60. "The Admiral," starring Robert Young, Robert Reed. Broadcast December 29, 1965. The admiral's wife dies, he tries to begin again and get along with his son.

61. "The Enemy on the Beach," starring Robert Wagner, James Donald, Sally Ann Howes, Torin Thatcher. Broadcast January 5, 1966.

62. "After the Lion, Jackals," starring John Saxon, Suzanne Pleshette, Stanley Baker. Broadcast January 26, 1966.

63. "When Hell Froze," starring Leslie Nielsen, Jane Wyman (Addie Joslin), Martin Milner (William Hedge), Steve Carlson, Jeff Corey, E. J. Andre, Jean Engstrom. Broadcast February 2, 1966; written by Alvin Sapinsley; original story by Wilbur Daniel Steele; directed by William Hale.

64. "A Small Rebellion," starring Simone Signoret (Sara Lescaut), George Maharis (Michael Kolinos), Sam Levine. Broadcast February 9, 1966; written by S. Lee Pogostin.

65. "Wind Fever," starring John Cassavetes, William Shatner. Broadcast March 2, 1966.

66. "Tell Them the Streets Are Dancing," starring John Vernon (Dr. Steve Wojeck), Patricia Collins (Marty Wojeck). Broadcast March 9, 1966.

67. "Brilliant Benjamin Boggs," starring Donald O'Connor (Benjamin Boggs), Broderick Crawford, Susan Silo, Jean Hale, Emily Banks. Broadcast March 30, 1966.

68. "The Sister and the Savage," starring James Farentino, Connie Francis (Sister Mary Clare), Steve Carlson, Anne Seymour, George N. Neise, Melinda Fee, Joseph Mell, Mimi Dillard, Michael Stanwood, Priscilla Boyd, Alan DeWitt. Broadcast April 6, 1966; written by Edward de Blasio, Dick Nelson; original story by Thomas B. Dewey; directed by Gerald Mayer.

69. "The Faceless Man," starring Jack Lord (Agent Don Owens alias Joe Smitty), Shirley Knight (Angie Peterson), Mercedes McCambridge (Frances), Jack Weston (Randolph Riker), Charles Drake (Dolan), Robert Pine (Ed), Joseph Wiseman (Rajeski), Don Hammer (O'Hara). Broadcast May 4, 1966; written by Steven Bochco, Harold Clements; directed by Josef Leytes. Additional film footage was added to this episode and it was released theatrically as *The Counterfeit Killer*.

70. "Holloway's Daughters," starring Robert Young, Brooke Bundy, Barbara Hershey, David Wayne. Broadcast May 11, 1966.

71. "One Embezzlement and Two Margaritas," starring Michael Rennie, Jack Kelly, Antoinette Bower. Broadcast May 18, 1966.

72. "Runaway Boy," starring Robert Wagner, Carol Lynley, Lola Albright, Sean Garrison. Broadcast May 25, 1966.

73. "Guilty or Not Guilty," starring Diana Hyland (Mrs. Collier), Richard Beymer, Robert Ryan (Andrew Dixon), Pippa Scott. Broadcast June 1, 1966; written by Evan Hunter. This was a potential pilot for Robert Ryan.

74. "Shipwrecked," starring Jason Robards, Jr., Hope Lange. Broadcast June 8, 1966.

75. "In Pursuit of Excellence," starring Glenn Corbett, Ed Begley, Joanne Medley, John Williams. Broadcast June 22, 1966.

CHRYSLER THEATRE SEASON 4

76. "Nightmare," starring Julie Harris (Isobel Cain), Farley Granger (Morgan Cain), Thomas Gomez, Joan Huntington, Elmer Modlin, Josh Adams. Broadcast September 14, 1966; written by Leslie Stevens; directed by Robert Stevens.

77. "Time of Flight," starring Juliet Mills (Mary Lewis), Jack Klugman (Markos), Jack Kelly (Al Packer), Jeanette Nolan (Mrs. Gardner), Woodrow Parfrey (DeCarlo), Michael Conrad (McWhorter), Peter Brocco (LQuar), Lloyd Haynes (Christensen), Clarke Gordon (Dr. Gardner), Bill Hart (Reed), Dave Morick (Max), Nancy Hsueh (Miss Chan). Broadcast September 21, 1966; written by Richard Matheson; directed by Joseph Sargent.

78. "And Baby Makes Five," starring Angie Dickinson, Cliff Robertson, Nina Foch, Walter Abel. Broadcast October 5, 1966; written by Hal Kanter; directed by Hal Kanter.

79. "Crazier Than Cotton," starring Jean Simmons, Kevin McCarthy, Bradford Dillman (Matt), Charles Aidman. Broadcast October 12, 1966; written by S. Lee Pogostin; directed by S. Lee Pogostin.

80. "Murder at N.B.C.," starring Johnny Carson, Milton Berle, Red Buttons, Don Adams, Bob Hope, Dick Shawn, Don Rickles, Dan Rowan, Dick Martin, Jack Carter, Soupy Sales, Bill Cosby, Jimmy Durante, Jonathan Winters, Bill Dana, Wally Cox. Broadcast October 19, 1966.

81. "Massacre at Fort Phil Kearny," starring Richard Egan (Col. Carrington), Robert Fuller (Capt. William J. Fetterman), Robert Pine (Lt. Brown), Carroll O'Connor, Phyllis Avery, Peter Duryea. Broadcast October 26, 1966. This episode was based on a true story.

82. "Dear Deductible," starring Peter Falk, Janet Leigh, Norman Fell. Broadcast November 9, 1966; written by Raphael David Blau; directed by Jess Oppenheimer.

83. "Fantastic Stomach," starring Jackie Gleason, Bing Crosby. Broadcast November 16, 1966.

84. "The Blue-Eyed Horse," starring Ernest Borgnine (Melvin Feebie), Joan Blondell (Mrs. Feebie), Ann Jillian, Paul Lynde, Joyce Jameson, G. D. Spradlin, Noam Pitlik, Eddie Quillan, Johnny Silver. Broadcast November 23, 1966; written by Michael Fessier; directed by Hal Kanter.

85. "The Fatal Mistake," starring Roddy McDowall, Arthur Hill, Marge Redmond, Michael Wilding, Alice Rawlings. Broadcast November 30, 1966.

86. "Storm Crossing," starring Jack Lord, Barbara Rush. Broadcast December 7, 1966.

87. "The Eighth Day," starring George Maharis, Mike Robertson, Barbara Barrie, Andrew Duggan. Broadcast December 21, 1966.

88. "Free of Charge," starring John Cassavetes, Diane Baker, Ben Gazzara, Pamelyn Ferdin, Suzy Parker, Johnny Seven. Broadcast December 28, 1966.

89. "A Time to Love," starring Deanna Lund. Broadcast January 11, 1967; written by Sidney Michaels; original story by Henry James.

90. "Code Name: Heraclitus (1)," starring Stanley Baker (Frank G. Wheatley), Leslie Nielsen (Fryer), Sheree North (Sally), Jack Weston (Gerberman), Kurt Kasznar (Constantine), Signe Hasso (Lydia Constantine), Ricardo Montalban (Janacek), Malachi Throne (Hoffman). Broadcast January 18, 1967; written by Alvin Sapinsley; directed by James Goldstone.

91. "Code Name: Heraclitus (2)," broadcast January 25, 1967; written by Alvin Sapinsley; directed by James Goldstone.

92. "The Lady Is My Wife," starring Jean Simmons (Mrs. Bannister), Alex Cord, Bradford Dillman (Bannister), L. Q. Jones, E. J. Andre, Begona Palacio, Lillian Bronson, Larry Watson. Broadcast February 1, 1967; written by Halsted Welles; original story by Jack Laird; directed by Sam Peckinpah.

93. "Blind Man's Bluff," starring Bob Cummings, Michael Rennie, Susan Clark, Farley Granger, Laurence Naismith. Broadcast February 8, 1967.

94. "A Song Called Revenge," starring Sal Mineo, Peggy Lipton, Kevin Coughlin. Broadcast March 1, 1967.

95. "The Reason Nobody Hardly Ever Seen a Fat Outlaw in the Old West Is as Follows," starring Arthur Godfrey, Don Knotts. Broadcast March 8, 1967.

96. "Verdict for Terror," starring Cliff Robertson, Michael Sarrazin (Darryl Cooper), Michael Constantine, Jo Van Fleet, Bettye Ackerman, Angus Duncan, Gene Lyons, Vernon Scott. Broadcast March 22, 1967; written by David Ellis; directed by William Hale.

97. "Dead Wrong," starring Patrick O'Neal, Tony Bill, Lynn Loring, Donnelly Rhodes, Charles Seel, Larry Thor. Broadcast date April 5, 1967; written by William Kelley; directed by Robert Butler.

98. "Don't Wait for Tomorrow," starring Juliet Mills (Princess), Telly Savalas (Mueller), Rossano Brazzi (Luder), Donnelly Rhodes (Matt Braid), Lily Valenti (Grand Duchess), Will Kuluva (Stassov). Broadcast April 19, 1967; written by Roy Huggins. This was an unsold TV pilot.

99. "Wipeout," starring William Windom, Shelley Winters, Fabian, Tom Tryon, Don Stroud, Les Crane. Broadcast April 26, 1967.

100. "To Sleep, Perchance to Scream," starring Ricardo Montalban, Lola Albright, Joanne Dru, Pat Hingle, Henry Beckman, Paul Hartman. Broadcast May 10, 1967.

101. "Deadlock," starring Lee Grant (Virginia Cloyd), Jack Kelly, Brooke Bundy, Tige Andrews, Donald May (James Lassiter). Broadcast May 17, 1967; original story by Ed McBain; directed by Leo Penn. Detective novelist McBain adapted the teleplay from his own story.

The Lucille Ball Show in episode "Lucy and the Plumber" (episode 3.2) September 28, 1964. Note: This was also the date that Hope's old friend Harpo Marx of the Marx Brothers passed away.

Have Gun Will Travel October 16, 1964

The Jack Benny Program appearing as himself in episode "Jack Makes a Comedy Record" (episode 15.5) first broadcast October 23, 1964

The Jack Benny Hour (1965); himself

The Andy Williams Show (1962) October 11, 1965

The Bob Hope Vietnam Christmas Show 1966

The Danny Thomas Hour (1967)

Get Smart appearing as room service attendant in episode "99 Loses Control" (episode 3.19) first broadcast February 17, 1968

Rowan & Martin's Laugh-In Episode 15 (episode 2.1) September 16, 1968

Rowan & Martin at the Movies (1968) himself

Rowan & Martin's Laugh-In Episode 17 (episode 2.3) September 30, 1968

This Is Tom Jones (1969) appearing as himself

Rowan & Martin's Laugh-In Episode 42 (episode 3.2) September 22, 1969

Jimmy Durante Presents the Lennon Sisters October 24, 1969

The Andy Williams Show November 29, 1969

Julia Episode "Cool Hand Bruce," 1970

The 42nd Annual Academy Awards (1970) Presenter, Best Documentary Feature, Best Documentary Short Subject, and the Jean Hersholt Humanitarian Award to George Jessel

Swing Out, Sweet Land (1970) Entertaining troops at Valley Forge

Raquel! (1970)

The Grand Opening of Walt Disney World (1971)

The Bob Hope Vietnam Christmas Show (1971)

The Odd Couple appearing as himself in episode "The Hollywood Story" (episode 5.4) October 3, 1974

Joys (1976) himself—In this offbeat comedy special, Hope satirizes the hit film *Jaws* with some top comedians being attacked by sharks. It is notable as one of Groucho Marx's final TV appearances. Groucho died in August of 1977.

NBC: The First Fifty Years—A Closer Look (1976) This mammoth special ran the entire prime time viewing period and featured some of the network's finest moments. A seventy-fifth anniversary show twenty-five years later, and hosted by Jerry Seinfeld, was much less interesting.

CBS Salutes Lucy: The First 25 Years (1976)

Barbara Walters Special (episode 1.3) May 31, 1977

Texaco Presents Bob Hope in a Very Special Special: On the Road with Bing (1977) Hope salutes his recently deceased friend Bing Crosby with a special about their Road pictures together.

The George Burns One-Man Show (1977)

The Muppet Show (1976) appearing as himself (episode 2.21) November 22, 1977

The 50th Annual Academy Awards (1978)

Bing Crosby: His Life and Legend (1978)

Happy Birthday, Bob (1978) Hope turns 75

The 32nd Annual Tony Awards (1978) (announcer, Irving Berlin Special Award)

General Electric's All-Star Anniversary (1978)

NBC Salutes the 25th Anniversary of the Wonderful World of Disney (1978)

Ken Murray Shooting Stars (1979)

Superstars (1979)

Bob Hope's Overseas Christmas Tours: Around the World with the Troops—1941–1972 (1980)

Lucy Moves to NBC (1980)

Bob Hope's All-Star Birthday Party (1980)

Bob Hope for President (1980)

The Bob Hope Christmas Special

The Bob Hope Anniversary Show (1981)

A Love Letter to Jack Benny (1981) Jack Benny's death from stomach cancer in December of 1980 prompted this loving and respectful tribute from an old friend.

The Bob Hope Funny Valentine Special

Spring Fling of Glamour and Comedy

All-Star Comedy Birthday Party from West Point (1981)

George Burns' Early, Early, Early, Christmas Special

Stand Up and Cheer for the National Football League's Sixtieth Year (1981)

Women I Love: Beautiful But Funny (1982)

Star-Studded Spoof of the New TV Season, G-Rated, with Glamour, Glitter and Gags (1982)

The American Film Institute Salute to Frank Capra (1982)

Unrehearsed Antics of the Stars (1984)

The Great Standups (1984)

Bob Hope Buys NBC? (1985)

The Kennedy Center Honors (1985)

The Bob Hope Christmas Show (1985)

A Masterpiece of Murder (1986)

Bob Hope's High-Flying Birthday (1986)

NBC 60th Anniversary Celebration (1986)

Bob Hope Winterfest Christmas Show (1987)

The Kennedy Center Honors (1988)

Highway to Heaven (1984) appearing as Syncompop in episode "Heaven Knows Mister Smith" (episode 4.23) March 30, 1988

We Can Keep You Forever (1988) (archive footage at POW homecoming)

America's Tribute to Bob Hope (1988)

Don Ameche (seated) and Hope, in his television movie debut, star as ex-adversaries who join forces to solve a string of underground art thefts and murders in "A Masterpiece of Murder" on January 27, 1986.

The Golden Girls (1985) appearing as himself in episode "You Gotta Have Hope" (episode 4.17) February 25, 1989

America's All-Star Tribute to Elizabeth Taylor (1989)

Entertaining the Troops (1989)

The Jim Henson Hour (1989) appearing as himself in episode "The Ratings Game — Miss Piggy's Hollywood" (episode 1.5) May 14, 1989

Sammy Davis, Jr., 60th Anniversary Celebration (1990)

You're the Top: The Cole Porter Story (1990) American Masters

Stars and Stripes (1990) (archive footage)

The Howard Stern Show (1990) The normally flippant Stern seems genuinely in awe at having Hope as a guest, while Hope himself, despite being 87 years old, appears to be enjoying the informality of the Stern program.

Roseanne (1988) appearing as himself in episode "Tolerate Thy Neighbor" (episode 4.5) October 15, 1991

Comedy in Bloom (1992)

Oscar's Greatest Moments: 1971 to 1991 (1992)

The Simpsons (1989) doing the voice for a cartoon of himself in episode "Lisa the Beauty Queen" (episode 4.4) October 15, 1992

Bob Hope: The First 90 Years (1993)

Laugh-In Past Christmas Present (1993)

Bob Hope: Happy 91st Birthday, Bob (1994)

Young Comedians: Making America Laugh (1994)

The Comedy Hall of Fame (1994) honoree

The Bob Hope Christmas Show: Hopes for the Holidays

Television's Christmas Classics (1994)

Radio Star — die AFN-Story (1994)

A Century of Cinema (1994)

Bob Hope's Young Comedians (1995) cohost

The Ed Sullivan All-Star Comedy Special (1995)

Bob Hope: Memories of World War II (1995)

Rosemary Clooney's Demi-Centennial (1995)

Classic Stand-Up Comedy of Television (1996) (archive footage)

Bob Hope: Laughing with the Presidents (1996)

Vaudeville: An "American Masters" Special (1997)

Bob Hope: Celebrity Bloopers (1997)

Bob Hope: The Road to the Top (1998)

Off the Menu: The Last Days of Chasen's (1998)

Cold War (1998) (mini) TV series (archive footage with Irving Berlin in Berlin, 1948)

The Best of the Dean Martin Celebrity Roasts (1998)

Songs That Won the War (1999)

Headliners & Legends: Brooke Shields (2001)

NOTE: There have also been several retrospectives about Hope's work in commemoration of his one-hundredth birthday, which took place on May 29th, 2003, and again upon his death that July 27th.

Many top comedians and sitcom stars of the period, including Kelsey Grammer and Conan O'Brien, as well as Hope's peers like Phyllis Diller, appeared on these salutes.

Afterword

When Bob Hope reached his hundredth birthday on May 29, 2003, there were tributes in newspapers and on television and a collection of his best Paramount films, all newly remastered, was released on DVD. On the occasion of his birthday, Hope quipped, "I'm so old they've cancelled my blood type!"

Then, on Sunday night, July 27, 2003, Bob Hope died peacefully in his sleep. He knew his time was running out, as did his family, so all were prepared for his farewell. Hope did have time for one last joke. There were several burial sites that welcomed Hope's remains, including some talk of Arlington National Cemetery as his final resting place. When his wife, Dolores, asked where he'd like to be buried, Hope quipped, "Surprise me!" This was only a week or so before his passing.

When his death was announced, all of the major television networks and cable networks offered tributes. Some independent stations canceled their programming and ran Bob Hope films. The news channels spent as much time discussing Hope's contribution as they would any world leader. President George W. Bush eulogized Hope as a "great comedian and great citizen." There were private funeral services for the family and closest friends, including Bing Crosby's widow, as well as a public service on August 27th, 2003, one month after his death.

Bob Hope's enormous contribution to show business will likely be represented chiefly by his motion picture work. His strong success on radio and television will probably be relegated to foot-notoriety in that his contributions to these mediums have not been made as readily available. With VHS, DVD, and broadcasts on cable movie channels, the films of Bob Hope will maintain his legacy.

In a 1980 interview the author did with comedian Phil Silvers, Silvers recalled his years in a "kid act" under the tutelage of Gus Edwards. In recalling Edwards, Silvers stated, "His name means nothing to you, right?"

It didn't.

"Well," Silvers continued, "some day people will recall 'The Great Bob Hope' and there will be youngsters who don't know who he is."

This seemed impossible or, at the very least, unlikely. Hope was so gigantic a figure in entertainment, even in 1980, that it seemed his name would be a part of our culture in the same manner as Elvis Presley or Charlie Chaplin.

However, there are indeed young people during the twenty-first century who may not have heard of Bob Hope. By the time he reached his one-hundredth year, he was no longer able to make any TV appearances (although it should be noted he was relevant enough to appear on the wildly popular cartoon series "The Simpsons" as late as 1992). And, sadly, most younger people do not bother to watch older films, despite their greater availability via VHS, DVD, and cable television.

As stated previously, none of the Bob Hope films is the sort of brilliantly constructed works of movie art as are, say, the films of Alfred Hitchcock, Orson Welles, or Chaplin.

Hope was not a director. His input was not cinematic. The directors he did use were those who could efficiently tell the story while spotlighting the humor. Directors like George Marshall and Frank Tashlin, to name two, have good credentials directing comedy films.

Hope's objective was to be funny and to provide a purely entertaining film for his mass audience. On that level he succeeded greatly.

However, there is a consensus that believes a film must have some artistic pretensions in order to achieve any level of lasting respect. This sort of thinking has resulted in the timelessly funny movies of Abbott and Costello or the Three Stooges being overlooked in most studies of comedy in order to concentrate on the work of masters like Chaplin, Buster Keaton, or Harold Lloyd.

It can be argued that the Hope films may be more accessibly entertaining than even the superior works by master screen comedians.

While researching this project, the writer naturally screened each of his feature films. In order to have a clearer perspective of his development and eventual downfall, the screenings were conduct in chronological order. It is perhaps difficult to clearly assess the earlier films like *Give Me a Sailor* while already having an understanding of the Hope persona. It was in development during this early part of his film career, and audiences of that time were not as fully aware of it as they would be today.

It does present the fact that even in his earliest B pictures, Hope had already exhibited a very natural, appealing comic style. He maintained it for a long period of time and used it as the centerpiece of some wonderfully funny films. *Road to Morocco, The Princess and the Pirate, Monsieur Beaucaire,*

My Favorite Brunette, and *The Paleface* all remain as fresh and funny as they were to audiences during the 1940s.

His weaker, later films, where his established style seemed out of place or a different variation was less successful, are easily obliterated by his many great movies.

The enormity of Bob Hope's tremendous stardom may not be recalled by future generations too young to have lived in his time. The timeless quality of his films — breezy, fast-paced, and genuinely funny — will serve as a lasting legacy and secure his name among the great movie comedians of the twentieth century.

Bibliography

Allen, Steve. *The Funny Men*. New York: Simon and Schuster, 1956.

____. *More Funny Men*. New York: Stein and Day, 1982.

Allen, Woody. *Woody Allen on Woody Allen: In Conversation with Stig Bjorkman*. Berkeley, CA: Grove Press, 1993.

Cavett, Dick, with Porterfield, Christopher. *Cavett*. New York: Harcourt, Brace, Jovanovich, 1974.

____. *Eye on Cavett*. New York: Arbor House, 1983.

Crosby, Bing. *Call Me Lucky*. New York: Simon and Schuster, 1953.

Faith, Steve. *Bob Hope: A Life in Comedy*. New York: G. P. Putnam, 1982.

Hope, Bob, with Carroll, Carroll. *I Never Left Home*. New York: Simon and Schuster, 1944.

____, as told to Martin, Pete. *Have Tux Will Travel*. New York: Simon and Schuster, 1954.

____. *The Last Christmas Show*. New York: Doubleday, 1974.

____, with Thomas, Bob. *The Road to Hollywood: My Forty-year Love Affair with the Movies*. New York: Doubleday, 1977.

____, with Shavelson, Melville. *Don't Shoot, It's Only Me*. New York: G. P. Putnam, 1990.

Lamour, Dorothy, as told to McInnes, Dick. *My Side of the Road*. New York: Prentice-Hall, 1980.

Lax, Eric. *Woody Allen: A Biography*. New York: Knopf, 1991.

Maltin, Leonard. *The Great Movie Comedians*. New York: Crown, 1978.

____. *The Great Movie Shorts*. New York: Crown, 1972.

____. *Leonard Maltin's Movie and Video Guide*. New York: Signet, 2003.

Manchel, Frank. *The Box Office Clowns; Bob Hope, Mel Brooks, Jerry Lewis, Woody Allen*. London: Franklin Watts, 1979.

Marx. Arthur. *The Secret Life of Bob Hope*. New York: Barricade Books, 1993.

Morella, Joe, Epstein, Edward Z., and Clark, Eleanor. *The Amazing Career of Bob Hope*. New York: Arlington House, 1973.

Nash, Jay Robert, and Ross, Stanley Ralph. *The Motion Picture Guide*. New York: Cinebooks, 1985.

Neibaur, James L. *Movie Comedians: The Complete Guide*. Jefferson, NC: McFarland, 1986.

Stoliar, Steven. *Raised Eyebrows; My Years Inside Groucho's House*. Iowa Falls, IA: General Publishing, 1996.

The Internet Movie Database (www.imdb.com)

Trescot, Pamela. *Bob Hope: A Comic Life*. Acropolis, 1985.

TV Tome (www.tvtome.com)

Index

4/18/16